# THE COUNTRY PRIEST IN
# ENGLISH HISTORY

The

# COUNTRY PRIEST

## in English History

## A. TINDAL HART
M.A. D.D.

PHOENIX HOUSE
London 1959

TO
Edward Richard Pitt Esq.
SOMETIME CHURCHWARDEN OF ST MARY MAGDALENE,
THORINGTON, ESSEX, AND OF ST JOHN,
HERNE BAY, KENT

© A. TINDAL HART, 1959

Printed in Great Britain
in 11 point Monotype Fournier by
C. Tinling & Co. Ltd, Liverpool, London & Prescot
for Phoenix House Ltd, 38 William IV Street
Charing Cross, London WC2

FIRST PUBLISHED 1959

# CONTENTS

# CONTENTS

# ILLUSTRATIONS

# PREFACE

THIS LITTLE BOOK on the country clergy does not pretend to the dignity of original scholarship. It is an attempt, based very largely on previous research into the life of the country parson, to evaluate the contribution he has made, along various lines of activity and in different fields of thought, to the making of English history and the building up of our national heritage.

I also hope it may help to draw attention to an urgent problem; one that should constitute a challenge to the whole of the Church of England: The country parson has been valued and needed in the past; is he still valued and needed today? If so, what steps are our diocesan authorities and country church laymen taking to preserve him? For the country clergy are a sadly bewildered and sorely worried lot of men in this so-called welfare state and atomic age. They are cruelly buffeted by the storms of inflation; they are watching the centuries-old village society of squire, parson, farmer, and labourer disintegrate before their eyes; and they are finding themselves saddled with the problems of crumbling medieval churches and dwindling congregations in the midst of a community where only money talks. And, indeed, from the Church's point of view that money is principally finding its way into the wrong hands—people with a long tradition behind them for getting and receiving, but little for giving.

On 17 May 1951 Mr John Betjeman published a brilliant little article in *Time and Tide* entitled 'The Persecuted Country Clergy', which aroused quite a storm of protest. He wrote: 'If he [the parson] is prepared to have a breezy word for everyone, give liberally of his small stipend to all funds and do a great many secretarial and transport and listening jobs free, his fence will not be pulled down, the church may sometimes be cleaned (for a fee) and he and his family will be tolerated. But if he teaches religion, if he attempts to be definite, if he administers and exhorts, if he really loves God and his neighbour fearlessly, he will be despised and rejected, when not actually mocked. Scandals will be spread about him and the witch-like malice of the self-righteous will fall on him.

9

The pride of the semi-educated, the anger of the greedy farmer will flourish in village sloth . . . the country parson's cross is heavy with their apathy and sharp with their hate. He sees his failure round him every day. Only the very few help him to bear it. Small wonder if sometimes he falls.'

These words may represent an extreme judgment; nevertheless they carry a moral and a warning.

*December,* 1958.                                    A. TINDAL HART

# ACKNOWLEDGMENTS

I am indebted to a number of friends, both clerical and lay, for help and advice whilst compiling this book. In particular I should like to express my thanks to the following: The Revd D. L. Scott, who read the MS and made many valuable and constructive criticisms; Canon P. B. G. Binnall; The Revd J. H. Jacques; The Revd Dr G. Soden; The Archdeacon of Newark; Dr H. E. Bracey; Edward Ingram Esq.; and to my wife, who compiled the index.

Thanks are also due to the following for permission to quote from the works named: the Oxford University Press for *Lark Rise to Candleford* by Flora Thompson; the Society of Authors and Dr John Masefield, O.M., for *The Everlasting Mercy*; and Jonathan Cape Ltd for *England's Green and Pleasant Land* by Robertson Scott.

# Continuity and Development

THE HISTORY of the English country parson has already been written many times and in considerable detail; and I do not intend to add to that story here—at least not directly. My aim is rather to show how in a comparatively humble and isolated sphere of life he was yet able to influence vitally, and sometimes decisively, the growth and development of the English nation in most of its aspects: religious, political, social, economic, and cultural.

The country priest and the country church have been existing in our villages from the very earliest times, springing up in the wake of the first evangelizing missions of Irish and Roman monks. Even if it is no longer possible to accept the theory that Archbishop Theodore consciously planned the parochial system in the seventh century, its creation must have begun at about that date, but in a rather more spontaneous and haphazard fashion. There seems little doubt that the lord of each manor, acting independently and on his own initiative, built a church on his land, appointed and paid its priest, and regarded the whole of the benefice as his own personal property. The incumbent's income was derived, apparently, from three main sources: a gift of land from his lord known as the 'glebe', which was often of considerable extent, and included as one of its privileges a freeman's rights of pasturage on the common and in the forest; the parishioners' dues and offerings, which covered a very wide and profitable field; and above all the tithe, which represented the annual tenth of the produce of the soil, the young of animals, and the labour of man, that was scripturally due to God, but normally paid to his servant, the incumbent of the parish[1].

This whole system of payment and appointment became very much more complicated and confusing after the Norman Conquest, when the successors of the original patrons of livings granted a vast number of their advowsons to monastic houses which, in the majority of cases, appropriated the whole of the benefice, seized the greater part of its tithes for themselves, and appointed a *vicarius*, or rector's substitute, to run the parish on a starvation wage, and with little or no security of tenure. However, at the Lateran Council

[1] See Chapter VIII.

of 1215 a canon was passed which gave to the vicar his freehold, and at the same time assigned him a reasonable minimum income. Furthermore, seven years later at the Council of Oxford it was decreed that he must be in priests' orders, or about to proceed to take such orders, and should reside constantly in his vicarage.

Yet in the long run this policy of appropriation proved disastrous both to the parochial clergy and to the parishes they administered. The Saxon rectors had often been men of good birth, learning, and culture, the sons or near relatives of the patrons, who served their people well in the combined capacity of squire-parson. The Norman lords, on the other hand, who succeeded to the manors after the Conquest, were the zealous founders or supporters of monasteries, handing over their advowsons to the monks under the mistaken but sincere impression that such unworldly regulars would prove better pastors than the secular clergy. In this they were at fault; for monks had little interest in or aptitude for pastoral work, and were concerned with their parishes only in so far as they could milk them of their revenues. The added evils of appointing minors— young children or students at the university—and foreigners to many of the remaining independent rectories further encouraged the growth of an ignorant and often peasant-born priesthood, men who either as *vicarii* or as *capellani* (assistant curates) could be used to fill the appropriated livings, parochial chapelries in out-lying hamlets, or the benefices of pluralist rectors and absentee foreigners. The *capellani* in particular were most unfortunately placed; since they were in receipt of little more than starvation wages and possessed no security of tenure whatsoever. In order to enable such men to be ordained at all there had to be frequent dispensations from canonical prohibitions. For example, candidates of servile origin and illegitimate birth, or those who suffered from some personal blemish or insufficient learning, were permitted to squeeze past the bishops into the Church.

All this was greatly resented in certain quarters. In his famous *Vision of Piers Plowman* William Langland depicted a clergyman named Sloth, who had been a parish priest for some thirty years, but was quite incapable of reading his service books properly; and voiced the general discontent when he wrote:

Now might each sowter [cobbler] his son setten to schole
And each beggar's brat in the booke learne.

John Wyclif, another critic of the official Church, condemned this type of priest for other reasons than his want of learning: 'The clergy', he said, 'haunten tavernes out of all measure and stirren lewid men to dronkenesse, ydelnesse and cursed swerynge and chydynge and fighttynge . . . Thei fallen to nyse pleies [foolish games] at tables, chess and hasard, and beten the stretis, and sitten at the taverne til thei han lost here witt, and then chiden and stryven and fighten sumtyme, and sumtyme neither have eighe ne tonge ne hood ne foot to helpe hem self for dronkenesse'. Poverty and absenteeism bred the abuse of plurality, i.e. the holding of more than one living by a single clergyman; and further lowered the prestige of the parish priest in popular esteem. He could not now hope to compete on equal terms with the wealthy, well-educated regulars or the eloquent friars; while his ecclesiastical superiors, the bishop and archdeacon, often treated him oppressively and arrogantly.

None the less, despite all his weaknesses, he remained a force of considerable spiritual power in the village; and throughout the entire Middle Ages wielded an influence over the peasantry that even the nineteenth-century squarson failed to emulate. Outwardly, certainly, there was little to distinguish him from the rest of the village community. He laboured with his parishioners on the open field, striving like them in good seasons and bad to wrest a living from the land; he was close to them in all the important events of their lives: baptism and marriage, child-birth and death; and inevitably in the tiny settlement of some fifty or sixty scattered households that represented an average village of perhaps three hundred souls, cut off by forest and swamp from the outside world, he became their leader and guide. No doubt his intelligence and learning were of a low order. He rarely preached a sermon, stumbled haltingly through the Mass, and was grossly ignorant of the scriptures. He dwelt in what was probably little better than a two-roomed hut, which he might have to share with colleagues, and where he was served only by the 'priest's boy'. Yet the aura of the priesthood surrounded him. He was the 'persona' of the village; and in times of sickness, trouble, or danger his people naturally turned to him for aid and comfort. An idealized picture of such a priest is to be found in Chaucer's famous portrait of the 'poure parson' out of the *Canterbury Tales,* who was described as 'rich . . . of holy thought and work', preached the gospel 'gladly', and taught his flock 'devoutedly'. He did not 'cursen for his tithes', but rather gave freely to the poor, whom he constantly visited.

> Wyd was his parish, and houses far asonder,
> But yet he lafte not for reyne or thunder,
> In sicknesse and meschief to visite
> The ferthest in his parisshe, smal and great
> Upon his feet, and in his hands a staf.

The 'poure parson' was not the man to hire out his benefice to

another, leaving his sheep 'encombred in the myre' while he himself
sought a chantry or some other lucrative post:

> But dwelt at hoom, and kepte well his folde,
> So that the wolfe made it not myscarye.
> He was a shepperde and no mercenarie;
> And though he holy were, and vertuous,
> He was to sinful man ful piteous,
> Nor of his speche wrathful nor yet fine,
> But in his teching discret and benigne
> To drawe folk to heven by clenenesse,
> By good ensample, was his busynesse:
> But were it any person obstinat,
> What-so he were of high or lowe estat,
> He wolde he snubbe sharply for the nonce.
> A bettre priest I trowe ther nowher non is,
> He wayted after no pompe nor reverence,
> Nor made himselfe spiced in conscience,
> But Cristes love, and his apostles twelve,
> He taught, and first he folwed it himselfe.

Up and down the country throughout medieval times there
must have been many such beloved priests; and despite all the evils
of plurality, absenteeism, and a sordid traffic in livings, the appointment of minors and foreigners, little learning, and gross poverty,
the country clergy played an important civilizing rôle in the nine
thousand rural parishes committed to their care. Each Sunday,
apart from any private offices he might say, the incumbent normally
conducted three services: Mattins at 6 or 7 a.m., Mass at 9 a.m., and
Evensong in the afternoon; and Langland demanded that the laity
should attend all three:

> And upon Sundays to cease, God's service to hear,
> Both Mattins and Masse, and after meat in churches
> To hear Evensong, Everyman ought.

By the thirteenth century he was also in the habit of offering up a
daily Mass. The ordinary rural clergyman was usually no preacher;
but he might catechize vigorously (a more effective method of
teaching simple people) and make good use of the occasional
offices—baptism, marriage, and burial, which were regarded as
events of considerable significance in the village—to drive home
the Church's lessons. These 'poure parsons' may have been simple
men; yet they did not fail to leave their mark on English history.
They became the spokesmen of the peasantry against the 'lord
monks', the lay nobility, or even the Crown itself in great national

uprisings like the Revolt of 1381. In the main, despite an anti-
clerical press that as in the case of the Great Plague of 1666 strove
to prove the abject cowardice and rapacious greed of the clergy
when faced by pestilence, they stood by their flocks during the
horrors of the Black Death, faithfully visiting the sick and burying
the dead, with the result that large numbers of them perished.
And afterwards they vigorously, if unsuccessfully, opposed the
enclosure policy of the fifteenth and sixteenth centuries, which put
sheep before men. Medieval village life was hard and savage; but
the lurid paintings on the chancel arch of the Last Judgment were a
constant reminder to the rustic worshipper that beyond this earthly
vale of tears, where the span of human life was all too often beastly,
brutish, and short, there lay the joys and terrors of Eternity.
Mother Church, moreover, in the shape of the parish priest, was
always there with her wise counsels and gracious ministrations to
guide his feet onto 'the strait and narrow path that leadeth unto life'.

This rôle of the 'poure parson', with of course the necessary
modifications dictated by period and circumstance, has persisted
almost unchanged into quite modern times. The parson continued
to live off the land. If, indeed, in a more prosperous age he did not
himself labour at ploughing, sowing, and reaping, the filling of
dung carts and the feeding of poultry and swine, he yet drew rents
from others who worked in his room and on his glebe. And if again
he no longer collected the tithes in kind and in person, driving his
cart from one farm to another and storing the proceeds in barn or
church tower, he was paid their equivalent in hard cash from the
same source. Furthermore, although from century to century they
might vary both in nature and in content, he still remembered to
take his surplice fees and to accept his people's offerings. He
remained the religious leader of the village, the *persona*, the maker of
its manners and morals. He persisted in acting as the champion of
his flock against injustice and oppression. His scholarship, usually
not very profound and rusting away in his country rectory, continued to evoke the awe of the yokel, who wondered how one
small head could carry all he knew. Above all, the tradition of the
beloved priest, the teacher, benefactor, father-confessor of his
people reigned unimpared from Chaucer's 'poure parson' to George
Herbert's 'country parson', Goldsmith's 'village preacher', and the
gracious, saintly, gentle rector of the type of R. W. Church at
Whatley in the Victorian golden age. That tradition naturally was
not invariably upheld. There have always been unsatisfactory
clergy: idle, ignorant, and worse. But the ideal was never quite
forgotten; it remained, as Herbert's country parson put it: 'a mark
to aim at'.

B

The position of the Anglican priest in his village was, of course, constantly challenged; and when at last the monks and friars were gone, Roman Catholics, Puritans, and eventually the various Protestant dissenting bodies took their place. Neither can it be denied that at certain periods in our history, as for example in the late sixteenth and early seventeenth centuries, at the time of the rise of Methodism, and again during the Reform agitation after the Battle of Waterloo, the parson was by no means a popular figure in the English countryside. Bishops and archdeacons have striven endlessly through their ecclesiastical courts to discipline and control the inferior clergy; but the deep-seated abuses of plurality, absenteeism, impropriations, and private patronage have all too often frustrated their efforts. The 'parson's freehold', too, in spite of its obvious advantages, has sometimes covered a multitude of clerical weaknesses and moral failings.

The continuity of these things, persisting substantially unaltered for nearly a thousand years from the Norman Conquest to the Great War of 1914-18, has undoubtedly helped to mould the pattern of English country life. Yet along with this continuity there have also gone important developments. At the Reformation the status of the country priest changed enormously; and although at first he may have instinctively battled against these changes, for he has always been a very conservative person, in the long run they led to his material and intellectual, if not his spiritual, betterment. Certainly by the end of Queen Elizabeth's reign he was very much better off than his medieval predecessor had been in such matters as housing and living-standards, education and social status. Possibly he was not quite so close to the soil or to his parishioners as in the past; but his eyes were now turning in another and upward direction. With an improved economic background, a recognized wife and legitimized family, he began to aspire to the position of a country gentleman. At first progress towards this goal was slow. Even in Queen Anne's reign his gentility was still a matter of some uncertainty and speculation; and he found himself in the equivocal and slightly ridiculous situation of being accepted in some quarters as a gentleman-by-profession, while regarded in others as an upstart or a menial. He might occasionally be permitted to sit down to dinner with the squire, but was always expected to rise again at the arrival of the pudding. Richard Steele, indeed, related the sad story of a domestic chaplain who had the audacity to remain seated and help himself to a jelly. He was later informed by the butler that his services were no longer required. However, the agricultural revolution of the eighteenth century, coupled with the Napoleonic Wars, so vastly increased the value of tithes and glebe rents that the squire's younger son was encouraged to take over the family living, and the gentility of the country parson was at long last fully and frankly admitted; with the agreeable result that the Victorian Age witnessed the golden summer of the parson's progress.

Let us then picture him in his prime as a resident country gentleman, the landlord of the glebe farm and the receiver of the tithes, who was usually also an extremely hard-working clergyman and a simple man of God. It must never be forgotten, of course, that there were plenty of indigent incumbents and some starvation curates about in the nineteenth century—the poor are always with us!—but the standard was set by the well-to-do rector of good family, who could meet his bishop or squire on the common ground of their social and intellectual equality. These men, graduates of Oxford or Cambridge, would employ a curate to do the rough work, whose stipend of £80-£100 per annum came out of the rector's own pocket; send their sons to the best public schools and then on to the university; spend long leisurely holidays abroad; mix in the best county circles; and dine not only with the squire, but frequently even in famous country houses, where they were certainly no longer expected to forgo the sweet. Absenteeism and plurality were at a minimum. In every village and practically in every hamlet there now stood a large, comfortable, and discreetly secluded parsonage, the interior of which was beautifully furnished, its library and larder adequately stocked, and its ample garden beautifully cultivated; the whole edifice resting securely on the backs of a large, efficient, but extremely badly paid domestic staff. Incomes on the average were very much smaller than those earned in the inflated currency of today, although their value in terms of goods and services, particularly in the country, was infinitely greater; but most of these better-class parsons and their wives also enjoyed some private means.

In conjunction with the squire, the rector ruled his village like a benevolent autocrat. Should the village inn grow too noisy in its cups he could and did turn its inmates into the street and order mine host to close his doors; and should a village maid offend against the moral law he might well cause the whole family to be evicted from their cottage and the parish. Many a village boy went to school clad in the cast-off raiment of the rectory; and when there suffered a flogging from the rector himself, which he may or may not have deserved. The school itself had possibly been erected and paid for out of the rector's own pocket; he controlled the appointment of the teachers; provided the prizes and treats; and saw to it that out of school hours it became the hub and focus point of a host of parochial activities sponsored by the parsonage. The incumbent, moreover, was not merely the master and father-bountiful of the parish, but also its protector and social reformer. One hears again and again of parsons who stood up for the agricultural labourers against the bitter opposition of the farmer, and provided them with allotments on glebe land. There were others who helped the more enterprising of their parishioners to emigrate; or who would coach the bright village boy for a university scholarship.

In so many ways, during these spacious and expanding years, the rector showed himself to be a pioneer. He started evening classes to teach the older men to read and write; organized savings banks, clothing and medical clubs; set up public libraries; revived May day revels and harvest festival suppers; and actually encouraged village outings, although for cultural rather than recreational purposes. 'We have watched', summed up the authors of *The Nineteenth Century Country Parson*, 'the practically universal establishment of residence, first insisted upon by parliamentary enactment, but later consolidated through the emergence of a new type of "reformed" country parson. We have seen him restore his church, tidy up its worship, and enlarge his rectory . . . some incumbents boarded pupils and most had private means. Near the restored church and rectory stood the new school, in which a fresh pattern of parochial life, with its constant round of meetings, clubs, readings and concerts had swiftly developed.' Parishioners came to their parson to ask him to make their wills and write their letters, to compose their differences, to intercede with their employers, and in fact to solve every problem that beset them whether material or spiritual.

All this was far too good to last. The financial stability of the clergy was undermined by the agricultural depression of the 'eighties and 'nineties; by an inflation which was engendered by two world wars and hit the small fixed income hard; by the agitation against the tithe that occasioned the Tithe Redemption Act of 1936; and by an increase in the number of ordination candidates without any private means of their own. The post-Reformation ideal of the highly educated country-gentleman-parson, who hand-in-glove with his squire was the master, reformer, and spiritual director of the parish, was practicable only so long as village life retained its cohesion and isolation. The invention of the internal combustion engine effectively broke down that self-sufficiency; while the rise of trade unionism, universal primary education, and the beginnings of the welfare state, slowly but surely put the three-fold leadership of squire, parson, and schoolmaster out of commission.

Another factor that made for the down-fall of the Victorian and Edwardian type of country parson was his ingrained toryism.

Socialist incumbents existed here and there; but generally speaking, and despite much philanthropy and liberal-mindedness, the average Anglican clergyman accepted the view that all change in the social system, especially that initiated from below, was to be deplored. Privilege and ownership, he was prepared to admit, ought to carry with them obligations towards the less fortunate sections of the community. Never the less, the failure of a minority to live up to their responsibilities was no reason, in the parson's eyes, for sweeping away the old order altogether. 'God bless the squire and his relations', he prayed, 'and keep us in our proper stations.'

Nineteen-fourteen is a landmark in English history as significant as 1066. For if the latter date introduced the continental type of feudalism into this island with all its complex relationships between master and man, which in one form or another has persisted almost unchallenged until the twentieth century; the former witnessed the beginnings of a social revolution, at present still only in its infancy, that is seeking to dissolve such relationships altogether and substitute other, as yet only dimly perceived ones, in their place. This gigantic upheaval has found the country parson on the wrong side of the fence; apparently wedded to the old order, but with his independence and initiative being steadily whittled away by the growing mass-production and bureaucratic methods that are infecting Church and State alike.

But before peering too closely into the thick mist that lies down the road and obscures his future prospects, it should prove both interesting and profitable to look into the long history of the English country parson and study the very real and solid contributions that he has already made to the society in which he has grown up.

It cannot be denied that the country priest has held a unique place in rural life. As the 'poure parson' he was always closely identified with the soil and those who tilled it; but as a country gentleman he also mixed freely with the best people in the land. A graduate of Oxford and Cambridge, he must at one time at least have moved in intellectual circles; while as a man of means he was probably well-travelled, besides being well-read. Often a born naturalist and nature poet, who might have said with William Wordsworth:

> There was a time when meadow, grove and stream,
> The earth and every common sight,
>   To me did seem
> Apparelled in celestial light,
> The glory and freshness of a dream

he was also the practical farmer and a man of business. A working parson, who laboured unceasingly to improve the material lot and intellectual abilities of his flock; he never forgot that underneath everything else, sustaining and inspiring them, was the priest, the mystic, the spiritual guide, the simple man of God. Secure in his freehold against dictation or oppression either from bishop or squire, with infinite leisure and every opportunity of developing his initiative and personality, his character might, indeed, soar into genius or degenerate into eccentricity; but, generally speaking, expanded along normal and healthy lines. Surely this man's achievements and failures could not help but leave their mark upon the English countryside.

> His virtues walk'd their narrow round,
> Nor made a pause, nor left a void;
> And sure th' Eternal Master found
> The single talent well employ'd.

# CHAPTER I

# Religious Leader

THE PRIMARY TASK of a religious leader is to give a lead to his flock in spiritual matters. This the country priest has usually done, although at certain periods of history he has been negligent of his duties, overshadowed or out-gunned by others in the same field, and sometimes held in but small esteem by his parishioners themselves.

Up to the Industrial Revolution England was predominantly a rural country; and outside of London and the universities, even in the larger and more important market towns and cathedral cities, community life remained based to a very considerable extent on rural lines and modes of thought until well into the eighteenth century. Over each little village with its manor house, farms, and huddle of rustic cottages towered the splendid church dominating the landscape and often the lives of its inhabitants besides. Here in medieval days the ordinary rustic worshipper was continually being brought face to face with the stark facts of coming death and judgment. For the church walls, particularly the chancel arch that displayed all the lurid details of the Great Doom or Last Judgment, were covered with bright paintings, which served as the poor man's Bible, teaching the unlettered peasant through his eye biblical and moral lessons as well as the stories and legends of the saints. Apart from these pictures there were the whole elaborate ritual of the mass, an occasional liturgical play depicting dramatically the Nativity, Passion, or Resurrection of Our Lord, and a rare sermon or catechizing, to help medieval man in his spiritual struggles against the World, the Flesh, and the Devil. Catechizing consisted of instruction on the Creed, Lord's Prayer, and Ten Commandments, and was used much more extensively by the average village incumbent than the preaching of set sermons.

Above all, of course, there were the intercessions of the saints, especially of the Virgin Mary; and the masses said by the Church after a man's death in order to secure his ultimate salvation. The mind of medieval man was, in fact, obsessed with and overshadowed by two things: the hope of Heaven and fear of Hell. Any help he could obtain that might at once improve his chances of the former and lessen the probability of his being thrust into the latter were eagerly grasped at. Hence the founding of monasteries, the endowment of chantries, and the saying of private masses. Under these conditions the parish priest, aided by his assistants, inevitably played a large and decisive part. Monks and chantry priests were all very well in their own sphere and place; but necessarily they could not and did not enter into the everyday life of the villager, for their functions were specialized and remote. Even the popular friars were come today and gone tomorrow. The parish priest, on the other hand, was always there, ready at any moment of the day or night to sally forth from his little house near the church in order to carry out his spiritual duties.

Almost immediately after birth an infant was brought to the font to be baptized, where in a long, elaborate service full of symbolism the evil spirit was exorcized and the child anointed and clothed in the white chrisom of innocence. Confirmation, too, was conferred at a very early age; and thus full membership of Christ's Church was achieved in the shortest possible time at a period of history when mortality among young children was extremely high. Much could also be made of the marriage ceremony, which concluded with the nuptial Mass and a visitation by the priest to sprinkle the happy couple in bed with holy water. However, the priest's most important duties probably lay in the hearing of confessions and the visitation of the sick. The sacrament of Penance for the Easter communion certainly entailed a great deal of work, since the priest was expected to conduct a thorough-going examination into the faith and morals of each parishioner, and to ask some very searching questions about their general behaviour and that of their children. The sick were visited constantly; and the clergy were strictly admonished to be always on the alert to perform this office. The actual visitation itself, indeed, was a very solemn affair, with the priest clad in his surplice walking from the church to the sick man's house, preceded by his clerk carrying the cross and lantern, and ringing a bell as he went. Communion must, in that manner, be brought to the seriously ill once a week, and unction once a year.

In such a fashion the parson was brought very close to his flock: presiding over the most important events of their lives, cognisant of their most secret thoughts, and guiding their feet along the paths of life and death. Furthermore, he would concern himself with their material as well as their religious welfare, their practical rearing as well as their spiritual upbringing. The priest, for example, was expected to warn mothers against over-laying or neglecting their children; and to advise them on all matters relating to the care and nurture of the young.

No doubt the ordinary village priest during the Middle Ages was ignorant and uncultured by modern standards; but in a village of illiterate savages, like the medieval villeins, his wisdom and knowledge were not likely to be questioned. In the valley of the blind the one-eyed man is king; so the medieval villagers were unlikely to cavil even at the parson who, announcing the coming festival of the Epiphany, once said: 'Tomorrow let us venerate Epiphany with deep devotion, for it is a very high and principal feast: I know not whether Epiphany was a man or woman, but whatever it may have been, this day must be observed by us with godly fear.'

Clerical examinations revealed very often an abysmal ignorance. One conducted by the Dean of Salisbury at Sonning in 1222 produced a mass of comments in the following style: 'amply illiterate', 'he is a youth and knoweth nothing', or 'it was found that he could not completely pronounce a single word of the Gospel or the Canon'. Neither was every country priest as orthodox nor as law abiding as the Church could have desired. John Wyclif, the fourteenth-century Rector of Lutterworth, was, of course, the outstanding rebel, who attacked in forthright terms the authority of both the Church and the Mass. With the assistance of some of his followers he translated the Latin Bible into English; and, collecting around him a body of disciples, most of whom were poor country priests, he sent them out into the countryside carrying copies of his Bible and preaching the gospel message with its corollary of a return to the simplicity and sincerity of primitive Christianity. These men proclaimed that the Bible alone mattered; it was the Word of God for His Elect, and his children should base their faith exclusively on its pages. Throughout the fifteenth century the Lollards, as these poor preachers were called, were sorely persecuted and many were put to death; yet they became the harbingers of the Reformation.

At the Reformation the rôle of the country incumbent was changed almost out of recognition. He no longer relied on symbols, pictures, plays, and ritual to instruct and impress his congregation. In fact he was now expected to condemn such things as superstitious. His church was drastically cleansed and his religious duties circumscribed by the Book of Common Prayer and the English Bible. His energies were mainly directed towards teaching, preaching, and praying, i.e. catechizing the young and servants; reading the homilies or preaching monthly sermons, if properly licensed to do so; and making regular use week by week of Mattins, Evensong, and the Litany. Holy Communion, on the other hand, was celebrated but rarely, perhaps three or four times in the year. There was also in puritanical or extreme protestant circles an insis-

tence upon the uniqueness and holiness of Sunday as opposed to
Saints' days and other church festivals, which they wished to see
abolished. Richard Greenham, the saintly Rector of Dry Drayton
from 1570 to 1590, declared: 'Our Easter Day, our Ascension Day,
our Whitsuntide is every Lord's Day. . . . For as the Jews used
the Sabbath as a day to remember with thanksgiving their creation;
so may we use that day for a thankful remembrance of our redemption, because in it we may meditate of all those benefits which our
Saviour Christ by his nativitie, circumcision, passion, resurrection
and ascension hath purchased for us.' Contrariwise it would have
been absurd to count every day as a Sabbath, 'as though we should
confound and shuffle together our working days and resting days'.
Sunday, indeed, to the Puritan had become equated with the Jewish
Sabbath, when all work and secular recreation must cease, and the
whole day be devoted exclusively to the worship and service of
God. Prior to the Reformation the custom had usually been for the
laity, once they had attended Mass in the morning, to feel themselves
free to do what they liked for the rest of the day. But the Puritan
now demanded that, when not actually in church, one's Sunday
should be spent in such practices as Bible reading, the giving and
receiving of religious instruction at home, the visitation of the sick,
and the distribution of alms. Sunday must be carefully prepared for
the previous evening by fasting; and the next morning, after a brief
private preparation, the whole household would walk to church,
silently meditating on the scriptures. During the very lengthy
service that followed, each member of the family was kept awake by
the knowledge that immediately after dinner he would be examined
concerning the sermon. Then the head of the house explained the
'main lessons of the Exposition'; and catechized his family until
such time as the afternoon service commenced. Dinner itself was
often shared with poorer neighbours or food parcels were sent out
'to the poor who lie sick in the back lane'. Finally, in the evening,
the sick themselves were visited before private prayer and meditation ended the spiritual labours of the day.

Puritan worship itself was strictly biblical, and embraced the six
ordinances of Prayer, Praise, the Proclamation of the Word, the
Administration of the Sacraments of Baptism and the Lord's
Supper, Catechizing, and the Exercise of Discipline. Greenham
wrote: 'Our hands are best employed when they are receiving the
Sacrament, our eyes when they are reading, our feet when they
bring us to the house of God, and our ears when we hear God's
word.' Puritan prayers were long and usually extempore; the
minister praying in a loud voice and the people assenting with an
even louder Amen. Prayer, declared John Bunyan, was simply 'a

groaning out of our condition before the Lord'; and it must be based on scriptural example and language. Praise consisted of the congregational singing of the psalms; and a psalm invariably concluded the communion service as it had done after the Last Supper. Preaching meant the proclamation of God's Word, the 'opening' of the scriptures, which were regarded as the supreme and final authority. Sermons were long, at least of an hour's duration, and two were expected to be delivered each Sabbath; while the reading of the homilies, which were regarded as mere moral essays, was strenuously resisted. The preacher's aim was 'conversion', to strike for a verdict in his listeners' souls; hence his message was simple and biblical, but exhaustive and prolonged, and was frequently accompanied by extravagant gestures. The catechizing of the young and of servants was carried on vigorously, both in church by the minister and at home by parents and masters. Discipline was strictly enforced, often for quite trivial offences, and in three well defined stages: the culprit was first admonished, then excommunicated, and finally, if impenitent, rejected.

Puritan churches were noted for their bareness and simplicity, with whitewashed walls and only a few scriptural texts for decoration. A high pulpit stood in a central position in the nave with a Bible resting on its cushion and the communion table immediately below it. Puritan worship, although it largely ignored the pictorial and concentrated on teaching and preaching, was by no means indifferent to sacramental devotion and did much by its reverence for scripture, its purity, simplicity, and spontaneity, its relevance to the life of its worshippers, and its protection of the Holy Communion against unworthy receivers, to raise the standards of morals and religion amongst the laity. Its defects lay in its often narrow-minded fanaticism, exaggerated fears of Roman Catholicism, and practical disregard for the wisdom of antiquity. Nevertheless the puritan country incumbent often became a real leader of his people. 'The Lord', wrote Richard Greenham, 'hath given unto the Ministers of his Gospel the power of binding and loosing both in the public ministry of his word, and also in the private consolation of his children'; while Richard Baxter declared: 'Every Thursday evening my neighbours met at my House, and there one of them repeated the Sermon; and afterwards they proposed what Doubts any of them had about the Sermon, or any other Case of Conscience, and I resolved their Doubts.' The minister in fact with his body of elders had power to enquire into the spiritual well-being of his flock, to admonish the backward, to suspend and even to excommunicate the 'unworthy'.

The Elizabethan Settlement put an end to an indiscriminate

destruction in parish churches; and by the beginning of the seventeenth century ornaments and ceremonies were slowly creeping back into the Church. It became the custom once again in many villages for the congregation to bow to the altar and to turn to the east for the creed; for the incumbent to wear his surplice with less objection, to chant the ritual, and to observe more regularly the authorized fasts and festivals. Communions were celebrated more frequently; water was mingled with the wine, a veil was used to cover the cup, and a credence table to contain the elements. New and fine stained glass appeared in the windows and illuminated texts on the walls. 'Much of all this was probably due to the example and widespread influence of Launcelot Andrewes, the saintly Bishop of Winchester, but also partly as a reaction against the dogmatism of the extreme Calvinists.' Under Archbishop Laud this process was carried a long stage further. Communicants were commanded to kneel in the chancel in order to receive the sacrament; the altar itself was moved to the east end and railed in; a cross and candles were placed upon it; and the congregation were expected to bow towards it on entering the building. The Arminian movement was now in full swing, attracting many erstwhile Roman Catholics and providing just that flavour of popery that caused its overthrow in the Great Rebellion. This new type of churchman was summed up by his enemies in a contemporary ballad of 1635 as follows:

> His Divinity is trust up with five points,
> He drops, ducks, bowes, as made all of joints;
> But when his Romane nose stands full East,
> He feares neither God nor beast.

Thus the twin streams of Evangelicalism and Catholicism flowed through our villages, gushing forth from the same eternal spring and having their source in the same delectable mountains, yet each cutting out its own particular channel and choosing its own path to the sea. The former was zealous in teaching and preaching the scriptures and passionately devoted itself to the pursuit of holy living and dying; the latter attached greater weight to an ordered Church worship, the supernatural in the Sacraments, and the beauty of an external symbolism with its strong appeal to the emotions. 'For the high Calvinist', wrote Canon Charles Smyth, 'the determining doctrine was election by God in his transcendant sovereignty, whereas for the high Anglican, it was Sacramental union with Christ incarnate in his Mystical Body.' Inevitably they were rivals competing for the soul of the countryman; at certain periods of history they clashed in open conflict: Puritan versus Laudian,

*George Herbert*

and Evangelical versus Anglo-Catholic; occasionally they would coalesce in a single great leader like William Law; but more often they would simply co-exist or even co-operate, each making its own particular contribution to the religious life of the countryside. The pre-Reformation Church could not fail to leave its mark on the mind and soul of the peasant, which time and change have never entirely eradicated; and indeed its teaching has now taken on a new lease of life with the sudden rise of Anglo-Catholicism that today vitally influences the Anglican Church. On the other hand in wide areas, particularly perhaps in the Midlands and East Anglia, the stern puritan spirit, hardened and fortified by persecution, is still very much alive: a creed that accepts the literal interpretation of the Bible, condemns the modern laxity of morals in no uncertain terms, demands the preservation and enforcement of the 'English Sunday', by which of course is meant the Jewish Sabbath, and is ever ready to cry out, 'No Popery'.

The two great examples of Laudian clergymen in the country are, one supposes, George Herbert of Bemerton and Nicholas Ferrar of Little Gidding. Herbert, the blue-blooded courtier, took Holy Orders against the advice of his best friends, who pointed out the mean social status of the average parson. But this was a challenge that he was fully prepared to meet. 'The domestic servants of the King of Heaven', declared Herbert, 'should be of the noblest families on earth.' His own ministry at Bemerton consisted of a ceaseless round of prayer and praise, of holy living and of holy dying. Communion was celebrated frequently; and twice every day at the canonical hours of 10 a.m. and 4 p.m. he conducted the daily offices in his private chapel, where 'he lifted up pure and charitable hands to God in the midst of the congregation.' The humble farm labourers working in the fields, Isaac Walton related, 'let their plough rest when Mr Herbert's saints bell rung to prayers, that they might also offer their devotions to God with him'. He ceaselessly visited both sick and poor, handing over a tenth of his income for their relief; and used to say: 'I would not willingly pass one day of my life without comforting a sad soul or showing mercy'. Herbert's remedies for the religious ills of his day were, first, the celebration of and teaching concerning the Sacraments; secondly, catechizing of the young in the liturgy and doctrines of the Anglican Church; thirdly, the preaching of gospel sermons; fourthly, the adoption of all symbols, ceremonies, and vestments approved by lawful authority, together with the solemn keeping of the fasts and festivals enjoined by the Prayer Book; and finally, a practical display of Christian living as a witness and example for others to follow.

In his famous book on the Country Parson he made his position quite clear in all these respects. On Sunday, he wrote, 'when the hour calls, with his family attending him, he goes to church, at his first entrance humbly adoring and worshipping the invisible majesty and presence of Almighty God, and blessing the people, either openly or to himself. Then having read divine service twice fully, and preached in the morning, and catechized in the afternoon, he thinks he hath in some measure, according to poor and frail man, discharged the public duties of the congregation. The rest of the day he spends either in reconciling neighbours that are at variance, or in visiting the sick, or in exhortations to some of his flock by themselves, whom his sermons cannot, or do not reach.' Catechizing was particularly valued by this idealized parson, since it infused 'a competent knowledge of salvation in every one of his flock. . . . He useth and preferreth the ordinary church catechism, partly for obedience to authority, partly for uniformity sake'. At home he must practise fasting, for 'as Sunday is his day of joy, so Friday is his day of humiliation'; while above all else the parson should be 'full of charity. . . . When he riseth in the morning, he bethinketh himself what good deeds he can do that day, and presently doth them; counting that day lost wherein he hath not exercised his charity.'

Nicholas Ferrar, the deacon of Little Gidding in Huntingdonshire, fashioned at its manor house a little religious community. This was no medieval monastery with its rules, vows, and discipline; but simply one entire family devoting its life to God in a ceaseless regular round of prayer and worship, study and work, charity and recreation, led and directed by a spiritual genius. Its faith and worship were based primarily upon the Gospels, Psalter, and Prayer Book; and combined sacramental teaching with the expounding of the scriptures.

A younger contemporary of George Herbert and Nicholas Ferrar was Jeremy Taylor, sometime Rector of Uppingham in Rutland, whose famous writings on such subjects as the Ministry, Toleration, Original Sin, the Sacraments, Public Worship, Preaching, and above all Piety, as it expressed itself in the individual religion of the soul, in the development of the Christian character, and in the practice and behaviour of Christian society, were widely read and approved by sincere Christians of all denominations, and exerted great influence for centuries to come. Indeed, in *Holy Living* and *Holy Dying* Taylor, although always a loyal son of the Anglican Church, had gone so far as to imply that sincerity in Christian living and an earnest striving after holiness in imitation of Christ were more important than a mere orthodoxy. 'Religion in a large sense', he

declared, 'doth signify the whole duty of man, comprehending in
it justice, charity, sobriety; because all these being commanded by
God become a part of that honour and worship which we are
bound to pay Him.' Further on he added: 'No pretence of Zeal for
God's glory must make us uncharitable to our brother'. Coleridge
once said that Milton and Taylor, despite their totally different
conceptions of churchmanship, yet agreed together: 'in genuis, in
learning, in unfeigned piety, in blameless purity of life, and in
benevolent aspirations and purposes for moral and temporal
improvements of their fellow creatures'.

Taylor's direct spiritual descendant was the non-juring William
Law, another country priest, who acted as chaplain to his lady
friends, Mrs Hutcheson and Miss Hester Gibbon, at the manor
house of King's Cliffe in Northants. Here, like the Ferrars of Little
Gidding earlier, they inaugurated a regulated life of prayer,
spiritual discipline, and religious exercises during the reigns of the
early Hanoverians and at a period of general moral and spiritual
apathy. This further attempt in a remote village, a century later than
the Ferrars, to revive the communal, devotional, and contemplative
life, is fully described in Law's best known work: *A Serious Call to
a Devout and Holy Life*. 'Persons of either sex', he wrote, 'desirous
of perfection, should unite themselves into little societies, professing
voluntary poverty, virginity, retirement, and devotion, living upon
bare necessities, that some might be relieved by their charities, and
all be blessed with their prayers, and benefited by their example'.
A community, moreover, that did not cut itself off from the world,
but lived in and for the world. 'Devotion', Law said, 'implies not
any form of prayer but a certain form of life, that is offered to God,
not in any particular times or places, but everywhere and in everything.' He then proceeded to describe in some detail what he called
'a profession of the soul'. 'Nourish it with good works', he cried,
'give it a place in solitude, get it strength in prayer, make it wise
with reading, enlighten it by meditation, make it tender with love,
sweeten it with humility, humble it with penance, enliven it with
psalms and hymns, and comfort it with frequent reflections upon
future glory. Keep it in the presence of God.' A proper and
consistent use of the sacraments, a regular round of public worship,
the setting aside of certain periods in the day for private devotions,
the need for daily confession and repentance of sin, intercessory
prayers for others, charitable works, and finally the cultivation of
the Christian virtue of resignation, provided in Law's eyes those
indispensable means of grace whereby, in accordance with the
teaching and demands of scripture, sinful man could build up his
soul and fit it for ultimate salvation.

The teaching of Jeremy Taylor and William Law had undoubtedly much in common with Puritans like Richard Baxter and even with John Bunyan, although ecclesiastically they were poles apart; and it is therefore scarcely surprising that their writings were instrumental in helping to determine the 'conversion' of John Wesley and the rise of Methodism, as well as influencing the Oxford Movement, whose reforming zeal began to permeate the countryside after 1845.

The Tractarians laid great stress on the Visible Church as the Mystical Body of Christ, which was at once Catholic and Apostolic, and dispensed the Sacraments as the recognized means of God's Grace. At a later stage Charles Gore, the heir of the Tractarians, referred to this Catholic Church as the 'Christ-bearer' and 'the Extension of the Incarnation'. To him, indeed, as Dr John Moorman recently pointed out, 'the Church was no other than the mystical Body and Bride of Christ, charged to carry on his work and to dispense his gifts to his people . . . the marks of the Church are three: Holiness, Righteousness and Authority'. The other great doctrine preached by the Tractarians was the Apostolic Succession, which alone could provide the Authority needed by the Visible Church; and must be wielded now and always by the Historic Episcopate, to whom alone had been committed the power to bind and to loose, to prohibit and to sanction. From these twin doctrines stemmed some remarkable changes in our country churches, that slowly but surely shaped the external pattern with which we are all too familiar today: the frequent and early celebrations, the wearing of the coloured stole, the lighted candles and crucifix on the altar, the robed choir, the chanted service, the revival of the Lady Chapel, the adornment of the interior of the church with ornaments and pictures, and above all the 'Catholic' sacramental teaching of the average country parson. The names of famous nineteenth-century high churchmen in country parishes, who blazed the trail and set the fashion, immediately leap to mind: R. W. Church of Whatley, R. S. Hawker of Morwenstow, Richard Seymour of Kinwarton, H. E. Manning of Lavington, and J. W. E. Conybeare of Barrington. The two last went over to Rome; and with the growing power of the ritualists and Romanizers there has been a steady Romeward trickle ever since. That was the cross and reproach Anglo-Catholicism had to carry.

Despite much common ground between such spiritual giants as Taylor and Baxter, Law and Wesley, the Evangelical stream ran over a very different course. George Herbert had written of the Puritan:

C

> She in the valley is so shie
> Of dressing that her hair doth lie
> About her eares.
> While she avoids her neighbour's pride,
> She wholly goes on th'other side,
> And nothing wears.

Only by preaching the Word of God in season and out of season, or so the Puritan maintained, could the truths of religion be really brought home to the hearts and minds of sinful men. Their preaching was supplemented by vigorous catechizing and diligent visitation; and their primary aim was to infuse 'enthusiasm', to effect 'conversion', and to drive home the one all-important lesson, 'To know nothing save Jesus Christ and Him crucified'. God had indeed chosen his Elect; union with Christ made salvation sure; and the assurance of salvation inculcated a resolute striving after holiness and perfection. The aim, in fact, of the Puritans, wrote Revd G. S. Wakefield in *Puritan Devotion*, 'was to bring "the labouring conscience peace" by the application of the Gospel of grace and holiness. They believed that the assurance of our standing with God is the great incentive to the spiritual combat'. Perseverance in the Christian life, leading on to ultimate perfectionism, was the sign of the 'saint'; with St Paul himself leading the way: 'I press toward the mark for the prize of the high calling of God in Christ Jesus'. Certainly no Christian has made a greater effort than the Puritan to relate his religion to the whole of his life, and to base it on his union with Christ and his overwhelming sense of the miracle of God's saving grace.

The Puritans and their successors, the Evangelicals, have often been accused of being philistines and spoil-sports. The hypocritical kill-joy, kneeling at his prayer-desk, with his high black steeple-hat tilted forward over his face to hide his grin as he pretends to say his prayers is a figure that has been assiduously propagated by the enemies of Protestantism, who would have agreed with Kenneth Hare when he wrote:

> The Puritan through life's sweet garden goes,
> To pluck the thorn and cast away the rose,
> And hopes to please by this peculiar whim
> The God who fashioned it and gave it him.

That was not true. The Puritans were well aware that relaxation was necessary. They loved good music, although they felt that its place was not in religion. In William Perkins's arresting phrase they were prepared to allow 'games of wit and industry'. For example, recreations such as shooting and fencing, running and wrestling, even chess, were permissible; but they feared pastimes like cards or mixed dancing that could so easily excite to lust and greed, to sin and damnation. Macaulay's famous taunt that the Puritan forbade bear-baiting not because it gave pain to the bear but pleasure to the people, was as false as it was unworthy. The Puritans were utterly averse to cruelty for cruelty's sake, and they were well aware of the evil passions this sport could arouse in the onlookers. Furthermore, although they had not the Catholic's love for and appreciation of the beauty and goodness of Nature, the Puritans were vividly conscious of the glory of God Himself, the Lord of Nature and the Supreme Controller of the Universe, before whom they fell down and worshipped. This worship was simple and austere, but it was also intensive and prolonged; something totally dissimilar from that of the Children of Israel at Mount Horeb in the Wilderness, who sat down to eat and drink, and then rose up to play.

The tenets of Puritanism undoubtedly took deep root in the English countryside: the love of Bible-reading; the wide-spread practice of family prayers and family religious instruction; the solemn keeping of the Lord's Day; the steadfastness under adversity, 'the Lord gave and the Lord hath taken away, blessed be the Name of the Lord'; the thrift, austerity and hard work; the reliance on Providence to bless and prosper the 'godly'; and above all, the strong, simple, moral outlook that refused in any way to compromise with sin or temptation, or what it was felt might engender both. These things still persist in our villages today, and date back to the early seventeenth century.

In the middle of the eighteenth century the Evangelical Revival carried the Protestant movement a stage further; for basing themselves on similar doctrines to those of the Puritans, the Evangelicals were convinced that the fall of Man's spiritual nature, due to the sin of Adam, could only be retrieved by the atoning work of Christ and the ministry of the Holy Spirit. The teaching of scriptural truths was still all-important; the primary objective was 'conversion'; and the subsequent progress of the individual Christian would be conditioned by the zeal with which he nurtured and nourished his soul in a 'religious society'. Thousands of these societies grew up in the country parishes of England during the latter half of the century, with famous evangelical parsons like William Grimshaw of Haworth, John Berridge of Everton, Henry Venn of Huddersfield, John Fletcher of Madeley, Samuel Walker of Truro, and Thomas Haweis of Aldwincle, leading the way. Many of these early pioneers became associated with itinerant missions. In other words they were not prepared to sit still in their parishes, when they felt their services were needed outside; and so they often wandered over the countryside preaching to all who would listen to them. However, their successors were better disciplined; and while less spectacularly successful, laid much firmer foundations in their benefices, where they remained intent on more solid and practical, if less emotional, ventures of faith.

Undoubtedly it would be true to say that the majority of the 'reformed' Victorian country parsons, who were responsible for the 'golden age' of the parochial system, were profoundly influenced by this type of Protestantism. The long biblical sermon, the lads' bible class, the 'moral' policing of the village, the inculcation of the need for spiritual discipline in the home, the denunciation of drunkenness and gambling, the unquestioning acceptance in spite of Darwinism of the literal inspiration of the scriptures, with all of which many of us were only too familiar in our youth, are eloquent witnesses of its potency. Certainly the unobtrusive evangelical piety of the average nineteenth-century country clergyman that suffered from no doubts or reservations, represented a tremendous power for good; one of the stabilizing forces which helped to create the greatness of the Victorian era.

This piety perhaps expressed itself most vividly at death, when the Victorian bed-room, with its large canopied four-poster bed, saw many a dramatically emotional scene played out to a finish. The Puritans had encouraged the practice, since it was their custom to surround the bed of the dying man with fellow-members of his congregation, who 'bent earnestly to catch the saints' last groans'. But for the full flowering of this gruesome rite one must turn to the diaries and reminiscences of the Victorians. In a long and beautiful account of the last illness and death of the Revd Edward Boys Ellman, Rector of Berwick in Sussex, his daughter concluded as follows: 'Warm milk with brandy was held to his lips, but he pushed it away. "No. Prayers first." Five minutes later after family prayers he could hardly touch it. . . . . At a quarter past 8 he tried to raise his head, looked up smiling, and said "Ready now" and moved as if trying to rise. . . . And so his gentle loving spirit returned to the God who gave it. Doubtless he heard the summons for which he had been longing for years; he had with patience waited for it, and when the call came for which he was ready and waiting, gladly answered, "Ready now!" in his last fully conscious moment ere he passed into the Valley of the Shadow of Death.' In the vivid account of his father's passing, recorded in his journal, the Revd George Powell of Hurdcott House in Wiltshire made sure of the dying man's salvation: 'I asked him if he had any fear of death. "No. No great fear." I enquired into his hopes of the future world telling him, with expressed quiet, that he must soon change this scene. He answered me in a longer sentence than usual in which I could only distinguish the words, "I have done my duty". I was anxious to know a more well founded hope than this —so I told him we valued not our works but were only accepted of God for the Merits of Christ. With more energy than I had yet heard him speak, he replied, "to be sure, to be sure". With regard to his spiritual state I was then quite happy. I shook his cold hand once. He knew it not.'

Scenes like the above must have been long remembered and treasured in the villages, where hopes of Heaven and fears of Hell continued to loom large in the peasant's mind. They also engendered a sense of submission to the Divine Will. Richard Seymour, speaking of the death of his first and newly born son, described how he and his wife 'prayed together for submission to His Will, and the continuance of His blessing and protection. . . . I have written all this thus fully for my own and dearest Fanny's comfort, in order that we may not forget the many interests and anxieties, the hopes and fears and joys and sorrows of these the first days of affliction that we have known since it pleased God to unite us as husband and wife. . . . Grant that we may be more earnest than we have yet been in doing the work appointed to us by our Saviour; I as a Minister of the Gospel, and my beloved wife as the companion, whom Thou hast given to me to share and assist my labour of love.'

Catholic and Evangelical parsons were not, however, the only ones to be found in our villages. From at least the time of Tom Fuller, the seventeenth-century historian and country parson, and possibly from that of William Langland in the fourteenth-century, if we dare claim him as a country clergyman, there has been the Broad Churchman or Latitudinarian, who has concerned himself with reason, morality, and practical Christian living, rather than with the nicer points of ritual and dogma. The judicious Richard Hooker, when at Bishopsbourne, used in his sermons 'to show reasons for what he spake; and with these reasons such a kind of rhetoric, as did rather convince and persuade, than frighten men into piety'. Fuller described himself as one who was at once willing to pray with the saints and play with the sinners. White Kennett, Vicar of Ambrosden and Rector of Shottesbrooke at the time of the Glorious Revolution of 1688, defined his own Latitudinarianism as 'quiet and efficient service to the Church'; while in a tiny country church near Windermere in the year 1789 a broad-church parson encouraged his flock in the following terms: 'Be ye virtuous; be active in your several occupations; be contented with your lot in life; be not envious of those that are above you, for they have their cares; which are greater than yours; be affectionate and charitable one towards another; love God as the Father of mercies; and enjoy those innocent pleasures which are within your reach, for this is the tribute most acceptable to your Creator. Be happy here, and trust in His infinite mercy for your eternal happiness hereafter.'

The nineteenth century produced some famous country priests of the 'Arnold of Rugby' school of thought: John Stevens Henslow, Rector of Hitcham in Suffolk, the Cambridge Professor of Mineralogy and Botany, was a brilliant teacher, who strove ceaselessly to develop the reasoning powers and observation faculties of his parishioners as well as their moral standards, social conscience, and love of righteousness. Then there was Charles Kingsley, the Christian-Chartist Rector of Eversley, who described 'saintliness' as 'a poor, pitiful thing, not God's ideal of man but an effeminate shaveling ideal'; and devoted himself instead to a practical, robust, muscular Christianity in his parish. Finally, out of many others, we might pick the name of the radical Rector of Stockton in Warwickshire, F. W. Tuckwell, who desired sweeping changes in the Establishment, whereby it would include all Christian sects. He published a pamphlet on the subject entitled: *The Church of the Future.* 'I contend', wrote Tuckwell, 'that a Christian Church exists primarily for the sake of the oppressed, the poor, the people.' The Latitudinarian and Broad Churchman stood four-square on the power of Reason; deprecating mysticism, miracle, and emotional 'enthusiasm', while boldly supporting the humanities, Christian morality, and practical Christian social service. God, to him, was a Benevolent Deity who functioned through natural laws; and he believed firmly in the need for a wider freedom within the Church, the comprehension of Dissent, and a reasonable liberty of thought and expression in theological and doctrinal matters. As Coleridge nobly put it:

> To walk together to the kirk,
> With a goodly company!
> To walk together to the kirk
> And all together pray.

These three streams of religious belief and expression: Catholic, Evangelical, and Broad Church, working side by side through the country clergy for over one thousand years, have inevitably helped to build up the English character. The sacramental means of grace, the stern discipline of the Puritan, the burning enthusiasm and converting power of the Evangelical, the liberalism and humanism of the Latitudinarian, have surely all played their part in creating a Comprehensive Establishment, wherein men and women have

learned much of Christian charity and love, a true fear and reverence of the Lord, the beauty of holiness, and a sound road to
salvation. Thus, despite the rapid growth of secularism and
materialism in this present age, the religious habits of the village
blacksmith and his fellow villagers have never been entirely out-
dated:

> He goes on Sunday to the Church
> And sits among the boys.
> He hears the parson preach and pray,
> He hears his daughter's voice
> Singing in the Village choir,
> It makes his heart rejoice.

What of the future? Will the country parson continue to lead his
parishioners in the things pertaining to the spirit? The answer can
be a convincing 'Yes', if he constantly bears in mind that ageless
portrait of the ideal priest drawn for us by the non-juring Bishop,
Thomas Ken, himself once a country incumbent:

> Give me the priest these graces shall possess;
> Of an ambassador the just address,
> A Father's tenderness, a Shepherd's care,
> A Leader's courage, which the cross can bear,
> A Ruler's arm, a Watchman's wakeful eye,
> A Pilot's skill, the helm in storms to ply,
> A Fisher's patience, and a Labourer's toil,
> A Guide's dexterity to disembroil,
> A Prophet's inspiration from above,
> A Teacher's knowledge, and a Saviour's love.
> Give me a priest, a light upon a hill,
> Whose rays his whole circumference can fill,
> In God's own Word and Sacred Learning versed,
> Deep in the study of the heart immersed,
> Who in such souls can the disease descry,
> And wisely fair restoratives supply.

CHAPTER II

# The Educationalist

DURING THE MIDDLE AGES, at least by the thirteenth century, it was a fairly easy matter for a poor but intelligent child to obtain an education; since practically every cathedral, collegiate church, and religious house in the country possessed its school. In addition there were the friary schools; and by the fifteenth century a large number of chantry priests, who besides singing masses for their benefactors were often expected under the terms of their foundations to instruct gratis the children of the poor. Consequently the gifted boy had every opportunity of climbing the educational ladder leading to a useful career in either Church or State. It was in fact regarded as an important religious duty to welcome and assist such children whenever and wherever possible; and in this charitable work the country priest began to play a part. For as A. F. Leach pointed out in *The Schools of Medieval England*, education 'was the creature of religion; the school was an adjunct of the Church, and the schoolmaster was an ecclesiastical officer. For close on eleven hundred years, from 598 to 1670, all educational institutions were under exclusively ecclesiastical control'. No doubt it remained a pious ideal that every country priest or his clerk should keep a little school under his own roof, where bright village lads could be grounded and coached before going on at an early age to the university or to one of the equally famous educational establishments at York, Canterbury, or Winchester. But none the less much was done in this way in the rural parishes, even if fees were sometimes charged or the teaching itself was of poor quality.

There was, of course, a certain amount of opposition to this free education of the poor. Richard II rejected a proposal aimed at forbidding villeins' children from being trained for the priesthood; and in the Statute of Artificers passed in 1406 it had to be expressly enacted that 'every man or woman of what state he be, shall be free to set their son or daughter to take learning at any school that pleaseth them within the realm'. When a boy reached the university at the tender age of fourteen or fifteen the full course of reading upon which he entered was a very long one. He would be expected to spend four years in studying his Latin grammar, rhetoric, and logic. Then, on taking the B.A. degree he would pass to the sciences: arithmetic, music, geometry, and astronomy, which gave him his M.A. Finally, if he so desired, he could spend a further seven years in learning theology for the B.D.; and three years more brought the crowning glory of the Doctorate. During the vacations these *pueri pauperi* would return home to work as labourers or perhaps turn beggar, tramping the countryside and asking for financial help at monastery or manor house. Many undergraduates were ordained into the minor orders of door-keeper, reader, exorcist, and acolyte, even the major one of sub-deacon, when still at the university; but for the sacred orders of deacon and priest they must first obtain a title, i.e. some place where they could not only exercise their ministry, but receive a sufficient stipend to maintain them financially whilst doing so.

The vast majority of country priests, however, had never been inside a university. They were illiterates, or at best had been very partially educated. Sprung from peasant or yeoman stock, they had contented themselves with picking up what crumbs of knowledge were possible from their incumbent, who was probably himself an unlearned and ignorant man. Taught in the elements of religion, they might then serve the priest at the altar, act as the parish clerk, receive minor orders, and gradually learn the services by following them carefully for a long time and making the necessary responses. That was the method by which many country clergymen were made. Langland condemned it wholeheartedly:

> The bishop shall be blamed before God, as I believe,
> That tonsures such of God's servants that can not sapienter
> Sing nor psalms read nor say a mass of the day.

Oxford and Cambridge, although they were making their influence felt more and more as time went on, could naturally only cater for very limited numbers; and consequently, in the thirteenth century for instance, many thousands of priests, who served the villages, must inevitably have been non-graduates. Furthermore, a university degree, unless the graduate also proceeded to his bachelorate and doctorate of divinity, which were usually only taken by men intending to remain at the university as teachers, was no guarantee that he was proficient in religious knowledge. Few country priests even possessed a Bible, which was often costly and difficult to obtain; and their knowledge of it was generally confined to some carefully selected portions. No wonder William Langland upbraided them for their ignorance:

> 'Ignorant fool' quoth Piers 'little lookest thou on the Bible,
> And the saws of Solomon seldom thou seest.'

For all that the ordination candidate really needed in order to qualify himself for holy orders was an ability to read his Latin Bible and service book, and to write reasonably good Latin prose. This necessary grounding could easily be provided by the local grammar school or, in only too many cases, by the country priest himself; particularly in remote and isolated parishes where any better education was hard to come by. He was expected to keep a school in his parsonage, to which any child could come either free of charge altogether or for what his parents cared to give. Inevitably, of course, the number of such children in any one village was strictly limited by the hard struggle for existence that went on continuously and demanded that every able-bodied man, woman, and child should labour ceaselessly on the land. Nevertheless an important and valuable part in the medieval educational system was played by the country parson or his clerk in the village school; they filled the gaps and provided the men that the Church so sorely needed to serve the rural churches and chapelries.

With the new impetus given to learning, both sacred and secular, by the coming of the Renaissance, the invention of the printing press, the translation of the Bible into English and the creation of the English Prayer Book, there arose a vociferous demand for a more learned ministry, a preaching and catechizing ministry that could adequately satisfy the voracious public appetite for biblical and doctrinal knowledge. The illiterate or partially educated priest of peasant stock, who had rarely preached or even catechized, and merely stumbled through the Mass in a language that few could understand, no longer sufficed. This type of man was, in Tom Fuller's arresting phrase, no more than 'the chicken of the Church, the sparrow of the Spirit', and was quite unsuited to a new and demanding age. On the other hand, the Puritan extremist could and did run too far in the opposite direction. The preaching of Robert Blackwood, an unlicensed minister, at Kirton in Nottinghamshire was, for instance, described as 'the roaringe of an Oxe in the toppe of an ashe tree'. Preaching and learning had to go together; and the Elizabethan episcopate set to work to achieve such a combination. Archbishop Parker, writing to Bishop Grindal of London in 1560, frankly admitted that in the past all too many men had been introduced into the Church, 'not traded and brought up in learning', and who were 'of base occupation'. So in his *Advertisements* of 1566 the Archbishop directed that the bishops and archdeacons were to examine their clergy, who did not possess an M.A. degree, at their next visitation and find out 'how they have profited in the Study of the Holy Scriptures'. Such a demand was renewed by Edmund Grindal in 1571, after he had become Archbishop of York. He told his clergy: 'Ye shall daylie read at least one chapter of the oulde Testament and another of the New with good advisement, and such of you as be under the degree of a maister of arts shall provide and have your owne, accordinge to the queenes majesties injunctions, at least the New Testament both in latine and englishe, conferringe the one with the other everye day one chapter thereof at the leaste.'

This policy of study and examination was vigorously enforced by most diocesan authorities; while at the same time every effort was made to increase the number of clerical graduates. Bishop Cooper of Lincoln, for instance, insisted upon ministers 'bending themselves diligently to the study of the Holy Scripture and Word of God . . . every day in the week'; and only B.D.s and D.D.s escaped the Archdeacon's examination. In the matter of graduates the Elizabethan Church was greatly helped by the rapid growth of the Tudor grammar schools, where the clever boy from any rank in society could pick up a good Latin education before going on to the revived and flourishing universities of Oxford and Cambridge. The bishops' overall report in 1603 for the whole of the provinces of Canterbury and York announced that out of approximately 9,244 parochial clergy, 3,806 held degrees of one kind or another, which was a tremendous advance on any previous computation of the ratio between graduates and literates in priests' orders. Soon, indeed, the universities were turning them out in such embarrassingly large numbers that the Church, with her limited financial resources, had difficulty in absorbing them all.

One of the first acts of Queen Elizabeth had been to forbid indiscriminate preaching; and henceforth only those who were licensed to do so might produce their own sermons. The rest must read one of the twenty-one authorized homilies. The number of these licensed clergy was at first small; but it steadily increased in volume as the years went by and the standard of learning in clerical circles rose ever higher. In the diocese of Lincoln the *Liber Cleri* of of 1576 recorded no more than fifty-seven qualified preachers and seventeen others who had preached without a licence; yet by 1592 the figures were very much larger, and not only in the diocese of Lincoln. Indeed, by the beginning of the seventeenth century there were, generally speaking, more preachers than readers everywhere.

According to the Royal Injunctions of 1559 the parson was expected to catechize 'upon every holy day, and every second Sunday in the year, to hear and instruct all the youth of the parish for half an hour at the least before evening prayer, in the Ten Commandments, the Articles of the Belief, and in the Lord's

Prayer, and diligently examine them, and teach the Catechism set forth in the book of public prayer'. These instructions were repeated with additions by Archbishop Grindal in 1571, when he ordered the clergy to catechize 'everye Sondaye and holye day', not merely the youth of the parish but servants and apprentices as well, 'both menkynde and womenkynde'. The parson was also told to make a careful note of any parents or masters who failed to send their children or servants or employees to church for that purpose, and denounce them 'to the Ordinarye'. Such demands were repeated *ad nauseam* in visitation articles and injunctions up and down the country. Catechizing was usually conducted on Sunday afternoons in church as part of the evening service; and its principal object, in the opinion of George Herbert, was 'to infuse a competent knowledge of salvation', and 'to drive it to practice, turning it to reformation of life'. He further argued that teaching of this type, which was based on question and answer, was superior to any other, since 'at sermons and prayers men may sleep, or wander; but when one is asked a question, he must discover what he is'. Certainly both Laudian and Puritan clergy alike enthusiastically adopted this method of education during the first half of the seventeenth century; although the Laudian stuck to his Prayer Book, while the Puritan based his teaching primarily on the scriptures.

Catechizing, however, was not only practised publicly of a Sunday in church, but privately during the week in the parishioners' own homes. Herbert's *Country Parson*, as has already been seen, spent part of his time: 'in visiting the sick, or in exhortations to some of his flock by themselves, whom his sermons cannot, or do not reach'; and in thus instructing his people he 'useth and preferreth the ordinary church catechism'. Lay folk who neglected to send their children to church to be catechized were punished. The whole of the parish of Hemingstone in Suffolk was presented during 1597 because the inhabitants had failed to compel 'their children, servantes and apprentyzes to com to church to be catechised for a year past'. Catechizing was undoubtedly taken very seriously both by teacher and pupils; and when at Helmingham, also in Suffolk, a boy was told that 'the dyvell was uppon his sholders', he promptly ran out of the church, 'crying and scryking to the terror of all that were presente'. Even after the Restoration catechizing was still regarded as the principal means of instructing the young in the elements of religion; and we find bishops, like Henry Compton of London, demanding of their clergy that they should 'restore catechising in all their churches in the afternoon'. White Kennett, who was Rector of Shottesbrooke towards the end of the century, wrote in 1698: 'Wee have settled the practise of frequent Communions; and keep a constant course of catechising and preaching every Sunday'. Thomas Bray, who became Rector of Sheldon in 1690, was a particularly zealous teacher of youth. At Sheldon he formed three classes of catechumens: those up to nine years old; nine to thirteen; and a senior group of all young people of fourteen and over. Each class was supplied with its own special course of study. Later Bray compiled his famous *Catechetical Lectures on the Preliminary Questions and Answers of the Church Catechism*, in four volumes. Their publication coincided with the issuing of Archbishop Tenison's Injunctions of 1695, one of which demanded obedience to the 59th Canon, and called for the regular catechizing of the young on Sundays. As a result Bray sold some 3,000 copies of his work, and made a profit of £700.

Meanwhile what of the village school? This continued in many parishes and was conducted by the incumbent himself or his curate. But occasionally the parish clerk or some other layman took their place. The Canons of 1571 had demanded that such *ludimagistri* should be licensed and must exhibit their licences at the Archdeacon's visitation. Otherwise they would be presented. The 78th Canon of 1604 had decreed: 'In what Parish Church . . . there is a Curate . . . well able to teach youth, and will willingly so do, for the better increase of his living . . . we will and ordain, That a licence to teach youth of the parish where he serveth be granted to none by the Ordinary of that place, but only to the said Curate.' However, he was not always willing; neither were his services always acceptable. At Bishop Redman of Norwich's Visitation of 1597 the curate of Glemham, the Vicar of Cromer, and the Rector of Hardwick were all presented for keeping private schools, where apparently they were charging excessive fees, and stifling any competition. The Vicar of Besthorpe and Rector of Gunton, who taught 'smale children' in their own parsonages, were likewise charged with similar offences.

Towards the close of the seventeenth century a new educational institution appeared: the Charity School. The newly founded Society for the Propagation of Christian Knowledge, led by enthusiasts like Robert Nelson, started these schools in London, from whence they spread out into the provinces. The charity week-day school, which was entirely free of charge, was paid for out of voluntary subscriptions, and its teaching was based almost entirely upon the Bible and the Catechism. 'Their object', wrote Dr Norman Sykes, 'was to give the children of the poor sufficient education to earn their living by manual labour and to read the improving religious tracts issued by S.P.C.K., without raising them above their station and producing an aversion to menial work.' Despite the fact that the Charity Schools were suspected of Jacobite activities, their numbers rapidly increased and many had become established in the villages by the early years of the eighteenth century. Diocesan bishops vigorously encouraged their country clergy to take them under their wing; but there were also many adversaries in the way. The bigger farmers almost to a man were bitterly opposed to a scheme which threatened to take the children off the land; and, in their opinion, would ultimately render them unfit for their proper function as servants and labourers. Then, unless the country parson was prepared to teach himself and pay for the school largely out of his own pocket, it was no easy matter to find properly qualified teachers, secure regular subscriptions from a tiny rural community, or even persuade the apathetic parents to send their children to the school at all. The indispensable preliminary condition, in fact, for the setting up of any such schools in the countryside was the creation of clerical societies; and there were simply not enough 'charitable' clergy to go round. Archbishop Herring's Visitation Returns in 1743 revealed that there were at least 266 villages in Yorkshire and Nottinghamshire where no school of any kind existed.

None the less, in many villages which contained an energetic parson or a socially-conscious squire, the children of the poor did receive some elementary education during the week in reading, writing, and arithmetic, besides religious instruction. This was all the more necessary because by the middle of the eighteenth century catechizing had largely fallen into disuse, or at best was only practised during Lent, in the summer months, or on the Sundays immediately preceding a visitation and confirmation. William Cobbett wrote in 1835 about catechizing: 'it does not exist: if it do, I should like to see the man that ever saw an instance of it. If anywhere practised once or twice in the year, it is such a rarity, so small an exception, as not to be worth naming'. Cobbett no doubt savagely exaggerated. But later still in the nineteenth century T. Mozeley, recounting his experiences as a country curate, spoke of a conversation he had had with a farmer about the confirmation of his daughters. 'I had tried them, but they could not say the Catechism or learn it. The farmer said he had never heard of any man or woman who could say the Catechism. "But", said I, "they cannot even say the Belief or the Commandments." "Nor can I", he said, "and I'm none the worse for it." ' This state of affairs, prior to the revival brought about by the Oxford Movement, was primarily due to the widespread practice of pluralism and non-residence that often obliged a single curate to serve two or three churches on a Sunday, and to gallop madly from one to the other, with only time for a brief service in each.

The Sunday School, which was started by Robert Raikes and Thomas Stock at Gloucester in 1782, provided a solution to the problem. For the Sunday School was a continuation of the Charity School idea, but on a less ambitious scale; and at the same time offered an alternative to catechizing. The teaching consisted mainly of religious topics, but also included the three Rs; and was given by qualified instructors, who were paid by means of subscriptions and donations. The leaders of the Industrial Revolution, now in full swing, who would have vetoed any revival of week-day teaching, when even the tiniest children were fully employed in mine or factory, welcomed the Sunday School, since they were only too thankful to see these dirty, savage little animals swept out of the streets and lanes of a Sunday into schools, where they were taught discipline, reverence, and cleanliness, and above all 'to do their duty in that state of life to which it shall please God to call them'. Parents, too, who had been indifferent towards or even hostile to the Charity School, accepted Sunday education with great enthusiasm; and their children flocked into the schools in ever increasing numbers all over the country, in urban and rural areas alike. Undoubtedly this public support for the Sunday School was to prove embarrassing in the long run, since Sunday came to be universally regarded as the most suitable time for instructing the children of the poor; and when full-time education was once again introduced in the shape of the week-day Church School, considerable opposition had to be overcome before it was accepted in many villages.

The National Society was founded in 1811 by Joshua Watson and his friends in The Society for the Promotion of Christian Knowledge; and between 1811 and 1834 contributed some £105,000 in grants for building new schools. At that date the then existing church village schools were often of the cheapest and simplest kind. The school might consist of a room at the inn or in a local farmhouse, the vicarage shed, a dame's cottage, or the church vestry; the teacher might be an ancient dame, a retired soldier or sailor, a hedge priest, anyone in fact who would accept the disgracefully low salary of £20 or £30 a year, without either board or lodging; and the children would attend only when they were not required by their parents and the farmers to work at home or on the land. When Charles Kingsley went to Eversley in the early 1840s he found the only school there was 'a stifling room, ten feet square, where cobbling shoes, teaching, and flogging the children went on together. As to religious instruction they had none'.

As late as the 1860s Rowland Williams at Broad Chalke near Salisbury had to contend with an old dame, who kept a school of sorts in her cottage next to the vicarage; where she beat her pupils with sticks purloined from the vicarage orchard.

In all too many cases, however, it was the clergy who alone kept the village schools alive; and the expense of first setting them up and then maintaining them fell almost exclusively on their shoulders. The government census of 1833 disclosed that a total of 1,140,653 children were then attending Church Schools; and Lord John Russell felt justified in accepting the voluntary system as a sufficient basis for a state grant. Accordingly a sum of £20,000 was voted for the maintenance of old schools and the building of new ones. 'No special machinery was set up to distribute the money', wrote Charles Birchenough in his *History of Elementary Education*. 'It was administered by the Treasury under a special Minute . . . no grants would be made unless at least half the cost were met by voluntary contributions; grants would only be made through the National or the British and Foreign School Society.'

The 'reformed' Victorian country parson certainly shouldered this task eagerly. He sought to establish as many schools as possible; raised funds for their building; found the teachers and paid them; and created in and around his schools a form of community life completely unknown before in the countryside. One of Her Majesty's Inspectors paid the following tribute to the clergy in 1842: 'I have looked carefully over my lists, and I can only find nine instances out of nearly 200, where I have not reason to think that the clergyman has a deep interest in his school, not shown only by words, but by watchful care and frequent attendance. I could mention instances, where, after morning religious instruction in the day school, the clergyman teaches the school at night; others where, when the master has been ill, or absent for some time, the clergyman has cheerfully supplied his place, lest the school should suffer loss; others again where, besides labour almost beyond his strength, pecuniary help beyond his means has been cheerfully given, poor children paid for, masters' stipends made up to a certain income, repairs done, as it were, by stealth, debts willingly taken upon himself, and contributions offered, liberal to excess, that others might be moved to contribute liberally.' Edward Boys Ellman in his *Recollections of a Sussex Parson* recorded how as Vicar of Wartling he started six dames' schools. His daughter later wrote of his work as Rector of Berwick: 'Berwick was made a model village. Each house was visited once a week, the school two or three times a day. Every child in the parish regularly attended Sunday and Day school. If a child were absent a single time, it was

Robert Raikes's first Sunday
School, 43 St Catherine Street
Gloucester, now demolished.

William Layng's Coaching Establishment at Creeton Rectory.

Portrait believed to be of Richard Hooker.

looked up at once, consequently, in after years the inspectors were amazed at the regular attendances. Sick people were visited daily. Night schools for men and lads were held each winter at the Rectory.' For the country clergy not merely built schools, but taught in them themselves for an hour or more a day. Normally they would give instruction on the Bible or the Catechism, but not invariably. J. S. Henslow at Hitcham took a botany class regularly in his village school.

The children were expected to pay a few pence each week for their education; and parents with large families and low wages often found this impossible to achieve. The Revd C. Richson, for example, declared bluntly: 'In a very large number of instances a parent has more than enough to do to provide sufficient food and clothing for his children'; and consequently secular instruction frequently continued to be given in Sunday School, because so many children had neither the time nor the money to attend week-day Church Schools. But this was by no means the only handicap the country parson had to contend with. The laity were often apathetic; the dissenters bitterly resented the fact that the village Church School was usually the only one available to which they could send their children; and the secular reformer began to clamour for state control in order to improve standards as well as to escape from denominational tyranny. The cry was also raised of 'educational destitution'. The Royal Commissioners of 1858 asserted that 11,024 parishes were without any school at all. At Takeley in Essex there were two schools, which the Vicar, Robert Hart, literally kept going single-handed in face of much bitter opposition. 'There was', wrote his son, 'a nominal committee, but its principal function appeared to have been to try and cut expenditure to the bone. At that date the government grant depended upon the annual examination, and a series of inefficient teachers at Takeley school in the early 'eighties almost caused it to disappear. Consequently the Managers had to find most of the money; and, under the circumstances, the Vicar achieved a great victory in persuading the farmers to submit to a voluntary rate.'

When the Revd George Gorham came to Walkeringham Vicarage in 1855 he found that all the managers of the school were dissenters and the master a local preacher. Some five years later the Vicar established the legal right of himself and his churchwardens to be the only proper trustees; and the Wesleyans went off in a rage and opened a school of their own. 'The National Church School' as it was now renamed, however, continued to give trouble; and after the passing of the Foster Act in 1870 was so badly conducted that the Education Department refused to recog-

D

nize it 'as an instrument of education'. This was largely due to an unsatisfactory headmaster and his wife, who were engaged to teach in 1872, but proved so violent in their methods of correction that they had to be dismissed. As no successor was immediately forthcoming, Gorham and his wife were obliged to do the work themselves. Richard Dawes of King's Somborne, who strongly objected to 'free' education, maintaining that an element of self-sacrifice on the part of the parents was essential, made on the other hand a great success of his schools, which were opened in 1842. It was, indeed, said of him that within the walls of his schools he achieved a moral reformation throughout the whole parish.

Undoubtedly the country parson had to maintain discipline and enforce a high moral code in an all-age school, where an inexperienced, timid, and probably uncertificated lady teacher alone presided. This he usually did effectively, but in a manner that would certainly not be tolerated today. Richard Seymour of Kinwarton was sent for by his wife, who was deputizing for the schoolmistress one November afternoon in 1840, in order to chastise an impertinent boy. 'I went', the Rector noted laconically in his diary, 'and flogged him.' Flora Thompson depicted a similar scene in *Lark Rise*: 'One afternoon, when a pitched battle was raging among the big boys in class and the mistress was calling imploringly for order, the Rector appeared in the doorway. "Silence", he roared . . . he strode into the midst of them, his face flushed with anger, his eyes flashing blue fire . . . he had the whole class out and caned each boy soundly, including those who had taken no part in the fray. Then, after a heated discourse in which he reminded the children of their lowly position in life and the twin duties of gratitude to and respect towards their superiors, school was dismissed.' Lee Warner, Vicar of Tarrant Gunville in Dorsetshire, behaved even more despotically. For on hearing during March 1882 that a boy at his school had committed an indecent offence against a girl; and then boasted 'of the same in filthy and disgusting language', he went straight to the boy's home, took him by force to the school and there administered a sound hiding. The Vicar was sued by the father; but the judge upheld his action, and fined him the nominal sum of one shilling for committing the technical offence of fetching the boy from his own home. The jury dismissed the case for assault. Lee Warner had stoutly refused to settle out of court. 'Of course', he wrote afterwards, 'going to the cottage was their best card, but really the battle I fought and not unsuccessfully was an acting manager's right to flog a boy when called to do so by the mistress in a bad case, in which she as a woman feels incompetent to deal with.' That kind of undisputed control by the country parson over his school was like a red rag to a bull where secularists of the type of Joseph Arch, the founder of the Agricultural Labourers' Union, were concerned; and helped to create the demand for an overall State and undenominational education.

A good picture of the benevolent but despotic rural Rector has also been drawn for us in *Lark Rise*: 'Every morning at ten o'clock the Rector arrived to take the older children for Scripture. He was a parson of the old school; a commanding figure, tall and stout, with white hair, ruddy cheeks and an aristocratically beaked nose, and he was as far as possible removed by birth, education, and worldly circumstances from the lambs of his flock. He spoke to them from a great height, physical, mental, and spiritual. "To order myself lowly and reverently before my betters" was the clause he underlined in the Church Catechism, for had he not been divinely appointed pastor and master to those little rustics and was it not one of his chief duties to teach them to realize this? As a man, he was kindly disposed—a giver of blankets and coals at Christmas and of soup and milk puddings to the sick.'

But it was not only in school hours that the nineteenth-century country parson sought to educate his people. For of an evening he would use the school buildings to instruct his adult parishioners. He held night classes there in the elements of education; gave lectures on history, the Bible, and the Catechism; and showed geographical slides in his new and exciting magic lantern. In a word, he had accepted the fashionable point of view that education was the panacea for all our ills; and heartily endorsed Bobby Lowe's famous remark, after the passing of Disraeli's Reform Bill of 1867: 'We must educate our masters'. Not of course that he ever dreamed that his own patient, subservient, rustic congregation would 'master' him. For the first half of the nineteenth century the idea prevailed in both Conservative and Liberal circles that education should either be controlled by the Church of England or else left to private enterprise. The Government, it was felt, should interfere as little as possible; and any sort of compulsory elementary education was a bad thing since it would probably make the poor discontented with their lot. Hence nothing was done directly by the State beyond subsidizing the National Society and the British and Foreign School Society, and establishing official inspectors, who, however, were controlled by the Archbishop of Canterbury. This was the golden age of the Church School, which in the village normally had no rival, and was to all intents and purposes the country parson's own private property.

Trouble began with the Revised Code of 1862, when the

Government grant was made dependent partly upon attendance and partly on the proficiency of individual scholars in reading, writing, and arithmetic, which was tested by examination. The last step was taken in order to put a stop to the system whereby the clever child received most attention, while the dullards were neglected. In other words the policy now adopted was one of 'payment by results'; and the clergy objected to what they considered to be the undue stress laid on secular subjects at the expense of religious instruction. Eight years later the Foster Education Act became law, with the avowed object of 'filling up the gaps'; since the voluntary schools were still only catering for about half the children of school age. The Bishops now made every effort to persuade their clergy, who had not already done so, to start up Church Schools in their parishes, and thus forestall the creation of Board Schools. Certainly the country clergy responded magnificently to this appeal; and, according to the National Society's own account, 'succeeded in doing in twelve months what in the normal course of events would have taken twenty years'. In fact, by the end of 1870 they had laid claim to some 2,885 building grants out of a total of 3,342. They also endeavoured to enlarge their existing schools and so increase the space for denominational scholars. Voluntary contributions for the work poured in at such a rate that some three million pounds' worth of new money was raised, while many existing annual subscriptions were doubled.

None the less, it was by no means possible, especially in districts where the Church was weak, to prevent the setting up of School Boards, which were often captured by secularists or extreme nonconformists; and gradually the State School began to assert its power in the countryside. Here the Bible was taught, but not the Catechism. The government grant to the Voluntary Schools was doubled; yet even so they found it impossible, dependent as they very largely were upon voluntary subscriptions and good-will, to compete successfully and indefinitely with an educational authority that could charge its expenses upon the rates. In 1880 elementary education was made compulsory; and eleven years later it became free. Henceforth, despite much increased government aid—for example by the Education Act of 1902 the local authorities were compelled to maintain the voluntary schools, apart from the upkeep of the fabric—the Church was fighting a losing battle, a financial battle, to save its schools. The controversial Butler Act of 1944, and the present frantic efforts to raise enough money to salvage at least a few thousand schools from the wreckage, is the logical and inescapable outcome. It must, too, be admitted that at any rate since the end of the first world war many of the country clergy have taken little interest in their schools, and have let them go without a struggle. Furthermore, it should be remembered that we are now living in a welfare state and a secular society that probably intends sooner or later to dispense with all voluntary and denominational elementary education altogether. It is, therefore, questionable whether it is worth the Church's while to spend a lot of badly needed money on their schools, which might be more profitably expended upon Church Teachers' Training Colleges.

But to return: the nineteenth-century country parson also advanced the cause of higher education by frequently taking in private pupils. Public-school boys who tended to stick in the lower forms, delicate boys for whom a boarding-school education was undesirable, and youths who wished to be crammed for the 'Little-go' or the Civil Service and Army examinations, would as like as not gravitate to a country rectory, where with plenty of servants to do all the chores and ample accommodation available, they were welcomed into the family, and provided the Rector at once with intellectual interests, congenial company, and some extra cash. The Rector of Creeton in Lincolnshire, the Revd W. Layng M.A., thus advertised his tutorial establishment in the year 1853;

Private Tuition.
The Revd. W. Layng, M.A.
Is ready to receive into his house Four Pupils to prepare them
for the University or Public Schools on the following terms:
Under 12 years of age     £60.
Above 12 and under 15   £80.
Above 15                         £100.
No extras except Washing.

A. G. Bradley described his own experiences in a North Devonshire rectory of the 'sixties, where the Rector, a notorious sporting parson, took in a few pupils: 'The fat boy and I had a definite and similar aim, which was to return to school two or three forms higher up, if possible. Our grasp of the dead languages was about on a par, and our hatred of them equally fervent, so we ran in double harness admirably, and sat together at table in the cheerful, sunny dining-room, worrying over the same books. . . . The Rector I am quite sure, hated teaching, though he played up most nobly and conscientiously.' On the other hand, it was not only the well-to-do rector, but the poor and learned curate who sought to supplement his meagre stipend in this way. 'Mr Walsh', recorded Francis Goddard in his *Reminiscences*, 'was one of those wasted intellects that one sometimes meets with, a double first class, many years curate at Tockenham at £80 per annum.' Walsh coached young men, Goddard among them, in mathematics for the 'Little-go'; and thus made his £80 go a little further.

The tiny, modern, and servantless parsonage of today is ill-equipped to cater for the coaching establishments of the past; much as their fees would gratify its present occupants. It is true that there are still some country incumbents, particularly ex-schoolmasters, in the old large rectories, who take in a pupil or two. In the Deanery of King's Cliffe not so long ago there was an enterprising parson who actually organized a full-blown crammers' college, where he employed a small staff of specialized teachers, charged high fees, and obtained good examination results. On the whole, however, the modern incumbent with high (and sometimes not so high) academic qualifications is looking for scholastic work outside his own home. He can, for example, give W.E.A. lectures in a neighbouring town, or teach at an adjacent preparatory school.

The English nation certainly owes a deep debt of gratitude to its country clergy for their splendid pioneering labours in the realm of elementary education, where in Charity School, Sunday School, and Church School they laid the foundations of the present universal and free education. Moreover, they have played no unimportant part in higher education by promoting the work of the endowed country grammar schools and preparatory schools. Above all, down the centuries, they have made it their business to seek out and train the scholar of the future. From the days of the clever village lads trained by their medieval priests for the Ministry, to those of the men sent to the universities or into the professions from the lordly Victorian rectory, there is a long and honourable record in this respect.

Can we say that it is now becoming a closed book?

# CHAPTER III

# Social Reformer

THE CHRISTIAN MINISTER must inevitably be a social reformer, since in this work-a-day world that is the only means by which he can hope to realize some of his ideals. Much of Christ's own teaching was of a socialistic, indeed of a revolutionary, nature; and all down the ages, despite Peter's exhortations to 'be subject to every ordinance of man for the Lord's sake', and to 'Honour the King', there has always been the Christian socialist, the rebel against the established system, or the Christian communist, who is not merely loath to render unto Caesar the things that be Caesar's, but demands that people should have all things in common. It is, in fact, curious that the so-called modern 'workers' should be utterly indifferent to the teaching and claims of Jesus, the lay-workman, who spent some thirty years of his life in a carpenter's shop at Nazareth, while they respond whole-heartedly to the call of an economist and philosopher, Karl Marx, who never worked with his hands at all. Why? The answer, perhaps, lies in the way in which Christ's official Church has reacted down the centuries to the needs of the working masses.

In the fourteenth century the Church certainly produced a social reformer of the first magnitude. His name was John Ball. Ball had originally been a priest at St Mary's in York, whence he had come to Colchester; and for some twenty years before the Peasants' Revolt of 1381 he had been stumping the countryside preaching against serfdom. William Morris in his *Dream of John Ball* described him as, 'clad in a long dark brown gown of coarse woollen, girt with a cord'. 'The man', he went on, 'was tall and big boned, a ring of dark hair surrounded his tonsure; his nose was big, but clear cut with wide nostrils; his shaven face showed a longish upper lip, and a big but blunt chin; his mouth was big and the lips closed firmly; a face not very noteworthy but for his grey eyes well opened and wide apart, at whiles lighting up his whole face with a kindly smile, at whiles set and stern; at whiles resting in that look as if they were gazing at something a long way off; which is the wont of a poet or enthusiast.' Such in imagination at any rate was 'the angry young man' of the age of Wyclif; a country priest rebelling against the social and economic conditions of his day. What had he to say? It was his habit, apparently, to wait outside a church of a Sunday morning and harangue the worshippers when they came out from Mass. 'My good friends', he would say, 'things cannot go well in England, nor ever will until everything shall be in common; when there shall be neither vassal nor lord and all distinctions levelled, when the lords shall be no more masters than ourselves. . . . They are clothed in velvets and rich stuffs, ornamented with ermine and other furs, while we are forced to wear poor cloth. They have handsome seats and manors, when we must brave the wind and rain in our labours in the field; but it is from our labour they have wherewith to support their pomp. We are called slaves, and if we do not perform our services we are beaten.' Here was the voice of the true revolutionary, the forerunner of Jacobin and Marxist; yet it was the voice of a Christian, and it certainly did not go unheeded.

Generally speaking the Peasants' Revolt was led by the laity and was as hostile to the official Church as to the landlords; but up and down the country other parish priests, like John Wrawe of Suffolk, followed Ball's lead, put themselves at the head of their congregations, and attacked their social superiors. Ball's own agitation had not gone unnoticed. He was excommunicated; and in April 1381 Archbishop Sudbury in a writ addressed to his Canterbury clergy described him as one who 'feared not to preach and argue both in the churches and churchyards (without the leave or against the will of the parochial authorities) and also in markets and other profane places, there beguiling the ears of the laity by his invectives'. Among others, Ball had attacked the Pope, bishops, and higher clergy, and demanded that no tithes should be paid to them unless the recipient was poorer than the donor. He was imprisoned again and again; and it was from Maidstone jail that he sent out his famous rhymed letters inciting his countrymen to rebellion:

> John Ball greeteth you all,
> And doth to understand he hath rung your bell,
> Now with right and might, will and skill,
> God speed you every dell.

Wat Tyler himself came from Colchester, where he had listened to John Ball's preaching; and when the rebellion started in real earnest it was decided that the hedge priest was to be the new Archbishop of Canterbury. The rebels broke into Maidstone jail and set him free for the historic attack on London. On Thursday, 13th June, the feast of Corpus Christi, Ball celebrated Mass for the peasant army arrayed in Blackheath, and afterwards preached an inflammatory sermon based on the text:

> When Adam delved and Eve span,
> Who was then the gentleman?

In this he urged them to stand together, not to be intimidated or side-tracked, and they were sure to win. 'By the word of that proverb he took as his theme', wrote the contemporary Chronicon Anglie, 'to introduce and prove, that from the beginning all men were made alike by nature, and that bondage and servitude was brought in by oppression of naughty men against the will of God. For if it had pleased God to have made bondsmen he would have appointed them from the beginning of the world, who should be slave and who lord. They sought to consider, therefore, that now was time given them by God, in the which, laying aside the continual bondage, they might if they would, enjoy their long wished for liberty. Wherefore he admonished them, that they should be wise and after the manner of a good husbandman that tilled his ground, and did cut away all noisesome weeds that were accustomed to grow and oppress the fruit, they should make haste to do now at the present the like. First the Archbishop and great men of the kingdom were to be slain; after, lawyers, justices, lastly whomsoever they knew like hereafter to be hurtful to the Commons, they should dispatch out of the land, for so might they purchase safety to themselves hereafter, if the great men being once taken away, there remained amongst them equal liberty, all one nobility, and like authority and power.'

John Ball had consistently demanded that England should be ruled only by the King and his Faithful Commons; and at long last this appeared to be coming true. He was doubtless also instrumental in drawing up the Peasants' Charter that demanded: abolition of serfdom, freedom of trade, cheap land, and justice for all. Ball, in fact, had anticipated by many centuries the slogan of the French Revolution: 'Liberty, Equality, Fraternity', and the Marxist cry: 'Workers of the World unite, you have nothing to lose but your chains'. He became the darling of the people; Archbishop Sudbury was beheaded as much for imprisoning him as for having introduced the poll tax; and for the few brief and terrible days during which the common people of England planted their feet on the necks of the mighty, the hedge priest was one of the leading figures in the rebel ranks. Then the forces of law and order rallied, and the revolt was put down with ruthless and systematic cruelty. John Ball himself was arrested at Coventry and brought before Justice Tressilian in St Alban's, where he boldly admitted the part he had played in the rebellion, confessed everything and retracted nothing; and was sentenced to be hanged, drawn, beheaded, and quartered.

So on 15 July 1381, the great rebel paid the price for his courage and
his failure. His quartered body was despatched to the four corners
of England to act as a grim warning to any would-be imitators.

In the last year of his life John Ball is said to have embraced some
of the tenets of the Lollards, who were likewise regarded as social
revolutionaries; although as a rule these poor priests never
attempted to incite the villeins against their masters, or instigated
any wholesale attack on property. Yet Wyclif and his followers
certainly objected to the payment of personal tithes to non-
residents; and their religious revolt, their own lives of poverty,
simplicity, and austerity, pointing the Church back to a Primitive
and Apostolic Christianity, kept the seeds of social discontent
alive right up to the Reformation.

However, for John Ball's true spiritual successors we have to
leap more than four centuries: to read the grim poems of George
Crabbe, and the satirical writings of Sydney Smith, to listen to the
voices of men like G. S. Bull, R. S. Hawker, Charles Kingsley,
F. W. Tuckwell, Edward Girdlestone, and Conrad Noel; and to
watch a thin trickle of parsonic indignation about conditions in the
factories and countryside swell into a flood of righteous wrath that
helped to sweep away such iniquities for ever.

In poems like *The Village* and *The Parish Register*, which he
described as the 'simple Annals of my Parish poor', Crabbe pointed
with a stark realism, that stood out in startling contrast with the
sentimental idealism of Oliver Goldsmith's *Deserted Village*, to the
evils of enclosure, the miserable wages often supplemented out of
the rates, the insanitary and overcrowded cottages, and the tyranny
of some squires and many farmers. Speaking, for example, of the
village poor-house he wrote:

> There children dwell who know no parents' care:
> Parents, who know no children's love, dwell there.
> Heart-broken matrons on their joyless bed,
> Forsaken wives, and mothers never wed.

*The Village* was published in 1783. Some twenty years later *The
Parish Register* appeared, which described how a village clergyman,
commenting on the entries of baptism, marriage, and burial during
the past year, frankly and sympathetically revealed the squalid
miseries of the agricultural labouring class.

Sydney Smith, a country parson par excellence, struck out for the
peasant in the *Edinburgh Review*. 'A labourer', he declared, 'with
six children has nothing to live upon but mouldy bread and dirty
water.' He was, however, the particular champion of the wretched
chimney boy and the even more unfortunate poacher. 'The hour of

dinner is short', he wrote, 'includes everything of sensual and intellectual gratification which a great nation glories in producing. In the midst of all this, who knows that the kitchen chimney caught fire half-an-hour before dinner and that a poor little wretch of six or seven years old, was sent up in the midst of the flames to put it out? . . . What is a toasted child compared with the agonies of the mistress of the house with a deranged dinner?' While of mantraps and spring-guns he cried: 'There is a sort of horror in thinking of a whole land filled with lurking engines of death—machinations against human life under every green tree and guns in every dusky dell and bosky bourn—the ferae naturae, the lords of the manors eyeing their peasantry as so many butts and marks, and panting to hear the click of the trap and see the flash of the gun.' Smith ardently supported Lord Grey and John Russell in their campaign for parliamentary reform and bitterly condemned the rotten boroughs. 'The happiness of the common people', he sarcastically affirmed, 'whatever gentlemen may say, ought every now and again to be considered.' In his own country parishes of Foston and Combe Florey he started allotments for the poor, fed and doctored them; while seeking to secure for their children some sort of education and training in the arts and crafts. At Combe Florey Rectory he kept an apothecary's shop which was always filled with drugs and groceries for the benefit of his parishioners.

R. S. Hawker of Morwenstow was another valiant fighter for the poor at the time when, in 1834, the Poor Law Amendment Act was passed, causing much hardship among the able-bodied labourers, who henceforth received no more outdoor relief to supplement their wages and to help their large families. 'They are crushed down, my poor people', Hawker declared, 'ground down with the wretched wage, the hateful truck system, till they are degraded in mind and body.' For at that date labourers were often paid in kind rather than cash and swindled into the bargain. Hawker started collections in the parish for their relief, which were roundly condemned by *The Times* as an encouragement to employers to continue to pay low wages. In an open letter to the proprietor, John Walter, Hawker retorted: 'I beg to inform you that the wages in this neighbourhood never fluctuate: they have continued at this fixed amount [seven shillings a week] during the ten years of my incumbency. Your argument is . . . because these labourers of Morwenstow are restricted by the law from any relief from the rate, therefore they shall have no charity from the Church . . . I have all my life sincerely, and not to serve any party purpose, been an advocate of the cause of the poor. I, for many long years, have honestly, and not to promote political ends, denounced the unholy and cruel enactments of the New Poor Law.' When, indeed, individual labourers came to him for advice, and had saved up a few pounds out of some wreck, Hawker told them to emigrate, so dark seemed their prospects at home. Speaking of the harvest of 1864 the Vicar wrote: 'I often think what heavy hearts there must be in the gathered fields— the toiling labouring husbandmen. They know well that the profit of all the increase is not for them, that they must still drag on life and labour to win their daily share of daily bread. There is not a clod in the furrow so hard as a farmer's heart. The very wages so hardly won they pay with grudging hands and they measure out the rates for the poor with strong reluctance—2/6 a week for the seven days food and clothing and fuel for an aged woman or man. How they live at all is a mystery.'

J. S. Henslow, Rector of Hitcham, also fought the local farmers to the death on this self-same issue during the hungry 'forties. He let out allotments on his glebe in face of strong opposition; and when at a meeting of the vestry his opponents banded themselves together and refused to employ any labourer, who held an allotment, on the ground that allotments created an independent spirit and undermined discipline, Henslow boldly threw down the gauntlet. He promptly let fifty-two allotments, and attacked the farmers in the press for their tyrannical behaviour. Indeed, he set such a hot pace that he quickly over-rode the opposition, who found they could not implement their threats, and won a resounding victory. At the time of the Rector's death in 1861 there were 150 allotment holders in the parish.

Richard Seymour of Kinwarton wrote in his diary on 26 October 1865: 'In the evening saw the men from the other end of the parish and allocated portions of the three acres let me by Sykes.' Seymour had long been the friend and champion of the poor. 'Went to the Alcester Board of Guardians as Guardian for Kinwarton', he recorded on 4 April 1843, 'did not like some of the proceedings which seemed harsh.' 'This evening', he noted on 14 October 1844, 'received the rents of my small tenants. They have paid well. The poverty-stricken and worn faces of many made me take their money with reluctance.' In point of fact he made it a rule to return the rent to those who were the hardest hit. Some clergy went further still and supported the Agricultural Labourers' Union, of whom Canon E. D. Girdlestone, 'the labourers' friend' was an outstanding example; and at the Union's first Congress a number of country clergy were on the platform.

Girdlestone had begun his fight for the farm workers at Halberton in North Devon during the eighteen-sixties, where he preached against the low wages paid and wrote letters to *The Times* on the subject. The farmers did all they could to silence him. They shouted him down at the Easter Vestry meeting, refused him a church rate, even left the parish church in a body and presented themselves at the Wesleyan chapel. None of these tactics intimidated Girdlestone, who organized an intensive and wholesale campaign of migration, sending between four and five hundred labourers and their families out of Devon into other counties where wages and conditions were very much better. Consequently the Halberton farmers had to raise their wages in order to keep their men; with the pleasing result that the seven or eight shillings a week of 1866 had risen by 1870 to seventeen. At the Church Congress in Bath in 1873 Girdlestone made a most moving speech on behalf of the rural labourers: 'When I think', he said, 'of that last great day, when we all meet together, rich and poor, learned and unlearned, master and servant, pastor and flock, for my own part I feel, and I feel it terribly, that the man whom I shall fear most to meet on that great day is the labourer.'

The West of England Labourers' Improvement Association, founded during 1870, originated in the village of Leintwardine with the active encouragement of the Vicar, E. J. Green. This Hereford-shire Union, as it soon came to be called, proved a great success, quickly spread to six counties, boasted a membership of 30,000, and secured an increase of 2/- in wages. Its first president was the Revd D. R. Murray, Rector of Brampton Bryan, who eschewed violent methods such as strikes, and relied instead on reason and moderation. This Union paved the way for the more militant National Agricultural Labourers' Union, which in 1873 federated all the then existing labourers' organizations and called its first Congress that same year. It was of this latter movement that James Lee Warner of Tarrant Gunville wrote in 1874: 'My own position in regard to it became (to myself) clearer and clearer. I always asserted *everywhere* the perfect right of the labourers to join the Union. I maintained that it was tyrannical to turn them off for so doing. At the same time I pointed out the limits of the movement, how it could not but depend eventually on the laws of demand and supply. Too much might be hoped from it as well as feared from it. I also told the delegates that I could not, as a clergyman to employers as well as labourers, go out of my way to urge the men to join the Union: at the same time that I was anxious to discuss the matter judicially with all who sought my advice and that they might have my word for it, that anything which seemed to me tyrannical should be remonstrated with.' In accordance with this last promise Lee Warner stood up for the older, respectable labourers of the vil-lage against Squire Farquarson, who seemed bent on refusing them work and turning them out of their cottages in the interest of more efficient farming, and to the tune of 'ye are idle, ye are idle'. 'Worms will turn', the Vicar informed him boldly, 'I do deprecate family men of good character of past fifty being driven out of the village.'

Conditions in the villages during the 'sixties and 'seventies were certainly very bad. Wages were often down to six or seven shillings a week; a chronic housing shortage existed, since landlords refused to build new, or even repair old, cottages; there was gross over-crowding; much malnutrition, which resulted in a great deal of illness, especially perhaps tuberculosis; and a very high mortality rate. James Fraser, who later became Bishop of Manchester, but was originally a country Rector at Cholderton in the diocese of Salisbury, speaking before a Royal Commission in 1870 on conditions in the countryside, said: 'Bread was dear, and wages were down to starva-tion point; the labourers were uneducated, underfed, underpaid; their cottages were often unfit for human habitation, the sleeping and sanitary arrangements were appalling. Naturally they took colour from their environment. . . . It was impossible to exaggerate the terrible state of things then existing; they were so bad physically, socially, economically, morally and intellectually that it would be difficult to make them worse.' The struggle went on; and inevitably some of these socially-conscious country parsons became politi-cians, although theoretically politics in the nineteenth century were supposed to be no concern of the Anglican clergy.

Apart, indeed, from a few parsons in the seventeenth century like Peter Simon of the Forest of Dean, who in 1631 was accused of preaching the equality of all mankind, the non-conformists had hitherto played the leading role in the realm of political socialism. During the Great Interregnum the more fanatical puritanical sects such as the Anabaptists, Familists, Levellers, and Fifth Monarchy Men had tried to put the Christian communist ideal into practice, led by men of the calibre of Gerrard Winstanley, the head of the Diggers, or George Fox, the founder of Quakerism. John Wesley, too, had not been indifferent to socialism; but with him conversion from sin and the claims of the after-life gradually dominated his thinking and teaching. Unfortunately for the Church of England the Evangelical Revivalists took the same line. They looked up-ward rather than forward; and although anxious for certain social reforms, notably the abolition of the slave trade, strongly opposed the revolutionary movements of the age. Wilberforce, for instance, worked against Trades Unionism, and even Lord Shaftesbury con-demned Chartism. None the less some of the eighteenth-century country clergy played an important part in helping to promote humanitarian schemes. James Ramsey, Vicar of Teston in Kent, published during 1784 an *Essay on the Treatment of Negroes*; and his account of West Indian slavery induced Lady Middleton of Teston Hall to persuade her husband Sir Charles to ask Wilberforce to press for a parliamentary enquiry on the subject. Ramsey was probably also instrumental in arousing Clarkson's interest in abolition while he was staying in the village as the guest of the Middletons.

The Oxford Movement did not at first ally itself with socialism. The Tractarians were concerned with the past: the revival of enthusiasm for the Catholic Church, the Sacramental System, and the Apostolic Succession. It was not until very much later that the Anglo-Catholic slum parson began to combine elaborate ritualism with red-hot socialism. However, lay socialists like Robert Owen and Richard Oastler found some supporters in the ranks of the country clergy. As early as 1795 Dr David Davies, Rector of Barkham in Berkshire, had written in his *Case of Labourers in Husbandry stated and considered*: 'In every nation the welfare and contentment of the lower denominations of people are objects of great importance, and deserving continual attention. For the bulk of every nation consists of such as must earn their daily bread by their labour. It is to the patient industry of these that the higher ranks are everywhere indebted for most of their enjoyments.' Then there was The Reverend G. S. Bull, Vicar of Brierly near Bradford, who campaigned vigorously for many causes: temperance reform, children's education, the Ten Hours Bill, and against the Poor Law Amendment Act of 1834. His short, thick-set figure was seen on a great number of platforms during the 'thirties and 'forties, where his sonorous voice and boisterous humour commanded attention. His appeal was always to hard-headed common sense and Christian decency. In all his writings and speeches Bull pulled no punches, and frequently called down upon himself the wrath of his fellow clergy. He was denounced as that 'pugnacious parson' and 'reverend bruiser'. Mr Gilmour of Halifax referred to him as a 'declaimer, consorting with the rabble and a participator in riotous assemblies and Bacchanalian orgies'. Another pugnacious parson was Dr Arthur Wade, Vicar of Warwick, who supported the Grand Consolidated Trades Union, and was once described as 'the only one of the beneficed servants of the Most High who had consistency and virtue sufficient to enlist himself in the cause of poverty and oppression'. Wade, a mountain of a man, led a procession of 50,000 people to petition the Government against the transportation of the Tolpuddle martyrs; and demanded that they should 'take the burden from the backs of the industrious and lay it upon the broad shoulders of the rich'. He added: 'to withold God's bounty from those who want, is the highest treason against Heaven.'

Another fighter on behalf of the working class was Lord Sidney Godolphin Osborne, Rector of Durweston in Dorset from 1841 to 1875, a philanthropist 'of a militant and almost ferocious type', who was Charles Kingsley's brother-in-law. Osborne wrote a series of letters to *The Times*, covering a period of more than forty years, in the interests of the Dorset labourers and other oppressed classes. His letter of 1846 spoke of 'a state of hideous moral and physical destitution' among labourers. 'Their wages', he declared, 'have been brought below the *minimum* of healthy existence and the poor-rate has forever to preserve a nice balance between absolute and partial destitution. The villages in which they dwell have been turned into dirty undrained lanes, bordered with hovel homes, whose outward evidence of physical want and filth form a speaking label of the moral destitution and moral filth to be found within; so crammed that the air in which the night's rest is sought is at least as foul as the conditions under which alone that rest can be taken. . . .'

The Reverend C. B. Dunn, curate of Cumberworth in Yorkshire, took a prominent part in the Co-operative Movement, for which he composed doggerel verses like the following:

> Let none who Christ's example court,
> Contend for sect or station,
> But all who human weal support,
> Support Co-operation.

The Reverend Joseph Marriott of Warrington was the chairman of the first Co-operative Congress in 1831, where he challenged the whole Church with the words: 'Can there be a more holy cause than this?' A later clerical advocate of co-operation was the brilliant high-churchman, Charles Marson, who wrote *God's Co-operative Society*. In a Somerset village Marson sought devotedly, untiringly, and not unsuccessfully, to forge a new and strong link between the Church and the real countryside of the rural worker.

Charles Kingsley, Rector of Eversley and the disciple of that fine Christian socialist, Frederick Denison Maurice, is a more controversial figure. On the one hand he called himself a Chartist. 'I am a Church of England clergyman', he said in 1849, 'and I am a Chartist.' But he was, of course, always a Christian Chartist, who deplored the aims of the wilder spirits. He signed a manifesto on behalf of the Chartists under the pseudonym of 'Parson Lot', and wrote his famous pamphlet: *Cheap Clothes and Nasty*. In conjunction with Maurice and J. M. Ludlow he started a new set of *Tracts for The Times* on Christian Socialism, founded a society for promoting working men's associations, fought a vigorous campaign

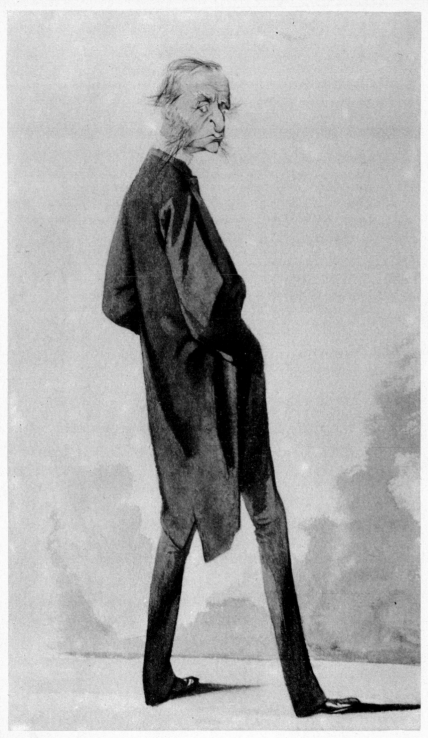

Charles Kingsley; by 'Ape'.

Sydney Smith; by Henry Briggs.

Richard Barham, author of *The Ingoldsby Legends*.

for better sanitation and a more efficient medical service in the countryside, and like Charles Dickens wrote novels—*Yeast* and *Alton Locke*—with the express purpose of forwarding social reforms. Yet Kingsley was never a true revolutionary. 'The only advice I can give', he once said to a working class enquirer, 'is, emigrate but never strike. . . . I am very sad about all these matters; but all I can recommend is, peace and making the prudent use of wages when they are to be got.' He was opposed to militant Trades Unions; for although he was an enthusiastic believer in helping the under-dog, particularly by means of sanitary reform and the preservation and enrichment of the land, he did not care for the idea of the under-dog barking and biting and helping himself. In the end it was his work as a clergyman and a naturalist that counted for most in his life.

A more resolutely socialist-minded country parson than Kingsley could ever have been, was F. W. Tuckwell, Rector of Stockton in Warwickshire from 1878 to 1893, who defined politics as the science of human happiness. Fifty per cent of England's population he affirmed 'were toiling, overworked and underpaid'; while some twenty per cent 'were living the life of beasts, ragged, filthy, famished, helpless, hopeless'. Religion, he believed, could not thrive on empty stomachs for 'starvation is a soil on which piety will not grow'. Yet he was well aware what would happen to a country parson who stood up for the agricultural labourer against squire and farmers, assisted in strikes, let allotments, and stood forth on platforms to denounce the tyranny of the mighty. His family would be ostracized in the neighbourhood; and his Squire would see to it that his church was emptied, his social activities thwarted, and the very men he was trying to help compelled to turn against him. Consequently most of the country clergy were afraid to criticize the slum conditions in their villages, and concentrated their attention on the souls rather than the bodies of their parishioners. At best they would salve their consciences by promoting charitable works, instead of trying to ameliorate conditions and raise wages. One rector's wife, indeed, used to open her weekly Mothers' Meeting with the prayer: 'O God, make these poor women contented with their lot.' In Tuckwell's view the Anglican clergy as a whole had failed. He demanded a more independent Church, and a more National Church that would include all the sects. 'On which side have they [the clergy]', he asked, 'shown themselves in any great and warrantable uprising of the masses? Are they not like lords and magistrates, the hierarchs of a privileged class?' He himself set great store by the secret ballot; and in the general election of 1885 attacked the landlords and farmers who were attempting to bring pressure to bear upon their employees to vote conservative. He was a great advocate of small holdings; and in his own parish let out the glebe farm on this basis. It proved a most successful venture; for by 1893 he estimated that some £800 was being taken out of the land and poured into the cottages in the form of bread, potatoes, pig-food, and other vegetables. His successor unfortunately ruined the entire venture by raising rents and cancelling the leases. Tuckwell spoke from platforms up and down the country on behalf of the Liberal party and against land monopoly and aristocratic privilege. He also played a part in the struggle for Home Rule for Ireland. In the course of his travels he met other radical parsons, notably Peter Young, Keble's old curate; but on the whole they were few and far between.

The fight was carried on into the twentieth century. A. W. Hopkinson, Rector of Winchfield in Hampshire, related in *Pastor's Progress* how from 1912 onwards he had done battle for the poor in his village: 'At Winchfield, from the first', he wrote, 'I had to fight the battle of the poor. And it was a single-handed fight; for no-one else dared to take part. It made my nine years there a very grim experience. But it proved that there is some advantage in the "parson's freehold". I was the only inhabitant of the parish who could not be turned out arbitrarily from his home. A blight of evil hung over the place: fear and suspicion made life a tragedy. All this aspect of country life came as a great shock to me. I had imagined that the days of tyranny were over, and that the workers had achieved freedom and independence. I quickly discovered how mistaken was this view.'

But if Charles Kingsley called himself a Chartist and Tuckwell a Radical, Conrad Noel, the founder of the Catholic Crusade and the aristocratic Vicar of Thaxted in Essex, would have nailed his colours to the mast of communism, a Christian communism of course. He stood definitely for 'a classless co-operative world of free men and free nations'; and he hoisted the red flag at Thaxted; but the inscription on it read: 'He hath made of one blood all nations'. Speaking of the type of worship he had instituted in his church there, Noel declared: 'We preach the Christ who all through his life stressed the value of the common meal, the bread and the wine joyously shared among his people, the Mass as prelude to a New World Order in which all would be justly produced and equally distributed.' Noel's communism in fact was that of the sheep in the parable, who were told by Our Lord: 'In as much as ye have done it unto the least of these my little ones, ye have done it unto me'; and represented Christian dogmatism rather than a political creed.

None the less a few swallows do not make a summer; and by and large it has to be admitted that the country clergy as a whole have always been conservative in their instincts and tory in politics. There was a grain of bitter truth in Charles Buller's witticism: 'For heaven's sake do not destroy the Established Church, it is the only thing that stands between us and Christianity'; and tory die-hards would hardly have disapproved of a pastoral sent out to his clergy by a late nineteenth-century bishop at the time of an approaching general election, which counselled them to abstain from party politics, but to do what they could to promote the return of candidates who were known to support the Church. 'There never was in the whole history of the Church of England', wrote the *Spectator* in September 1873, 'anything so unfortunate as the attitude the Clergy seem to be adopting towards the Labourers and their Union.' The reasons put forward to excuse or justify this attitude of either hostility or at best neutrality towards the reason-able demands of the farm workers, included the following: Christ-ianity, it was argued, was exclusively concerned with spiritual matters; the Church ought not to take sides; agitation or strikes were not needed in order to win improved social conditions; the Labourers' Union was led by an embittered nonconformist, who was known to be violently hostile to the Establishment; and, above all, the country clergyman's own economic interests as the owner of glebe and the receiver of tithes were bound up in the preserva-tion of the status quo. Consequently the average country parson was intensely suspicious of change; since change almost invariably worked to his financial disadvantage, as in the sixteenth and seven-teenth centuries, and again in the twentieth.

The Reformation, for instance, caused much dislocation in rural areas and greatly troubled the waters of clerical life. It was no coincidence that the clergy took a prominent part in the formidable Pilgrimage of Grace against Henry VIII, and in the Insurrection of the West against his son, Edward, in order to try to restore the *ancien régime*. For revolution nearly always takes an anti-clerical form; and the Reformation was no exception to this rule. One of the demands of Kett's Norfolk rebels in 1550 was that tithes should be abolished; and this became a constant cry of the Protestant extrem-ists. But when the Elizabethan Settlement had again given stability and security to the Church, the country clergy at once rallied to its support in opposition to the Puritans, who through their proposed Book of Discipline and Presbyterian system were threatening the parson's independence. 'No Bishop, no King', declared James I; and the parochial clergy might have added: 'no bishop, no freehold'. Consequently they supported Charles I against Parliament; not so much for his Stuart blood as because he represented a solid bulwark against disruption and nonconformity. And it was this underlying need for stability and continuity that drove them eventually to discard their cherished principles of the Divine Right of Kings and non-resistence to their commands, to attack vigorously James II's Romanizing policies from their pulpits, to refuse to read his Declaration of Indulgence in their churches, and to welcome the Dutch invader in his place. During the troubled years that followed the revolution of 1688—years in which the country clergy took a leading part in politics—the self-same motives and instincts were seen at work. Francis Atterbury and his friends in the Lower House of Convocation, and the bucolic parsons who cheered Dr Sacheverell to the echo, were alike opposed to the whig lords and the latitudinarian bishops, whom they suspected, not unjustly, of favouring the commercial and nonconformist interests at the expense of the landowners and the high flying churchmen.

Georgian England, whose agricultural revolution benefited the squire, the bigger farmer, and the parson at the cost of impoverishing the peasants and the landless labourers, confirmed and deepened this die-hard conservatism among the country clergy. It brought them into conflict with Methodism and Evangelicalism; and despite the great reforming movements of the nineteenth century, the Evangelical Revival and the Oxford Movement, the Victorian country parson remained a staunch tory, as stalwart an opponent of change and disruption, of socialist objectives and nonconformist claims, as ever his predecessors had been.

In the eighteenth and nineteenth centuries, as a member of the manorial class, the clerical Justice of the Peace became an important figure on the county bench; and not infrequently acted as chairman of quarter sessions. Here he usually upheld the interests of the higher as opposed to the lower stratum of society. In 1833 Francis Lundy, Rector of Lockington, despite the Act of 2 and 3 Ed. VI, summoned a labourer, Jeremiah Dodsworth, before two magistrates for refusing to pay personal tithes on his wages at the rate of 4d. in the pound. One of these magistrates was John Blanchard, a country parson. Dodsworth was ordered to pay the 4s. 4d. he owed, plus the costs of the prosecution; and on his refusal a warrant of distress was issued against his goods and chattels. But since he had none, John Blanchard, on his own responsibility, committed him to the House of Correction at Beverley, 'there to be kept for the space of three calendar months as punishment for not paying his tithes'. An even worse example of such clerical tyranny was seen at Chipping Norton in 1873, where parson magistrates sentenced sixteen women, some of whom were nursing children, to seven or ten days hard labour because, during a lock-out at Ascot in Berkshire, they had attempted to intimidate strike-breakers brought in by the farmers from outside. As a result of these and similar cases, an agitation was started to bar the clergy from the commissions of the peace; and although no actual legislation was introduced into Parliament, the number of clerical Justices of the Peace declined from 1,187 in 1873 to a mere thirty in 1903.

The country parson's strong counter to socialism was organized charity—the opium of the people—whereby in exchange for loaves and fishes the labourers might be prepared to sell their souls. *The London Daily News* once remarked of the Hon. J. W. Leigh, Vicar of Stoneleigh, that he was 'the brother of the Lord of the Manor and the Father of his parish. . . . In Stoneleigh Hodge indeed wears the collar of villein-ship, but it is padded inside and nicely gilt.' This charity expressed itself in a multiplicity of ways: straight-forward giving, the founding of clubs of every description, the running of concerts and penny-readings, the establishment of schools, the starting up of night classes and lantern lectures, the provision of village teas, suppers, and garden parties; anything and everything in fact that would prevent the farm worker from getting a square deal from his employer and landlord, the working class as a whole from acquiring any sort of real independence, and the non-conformist minister from securing parity of treatment with the Rector. Joseph Arch, the founder of the Agricultural Labourers' Union, had deserted the Church for the Chapel because a village parson and his wife had refused soup and coal to his mother since she was not 'properly humble' enough. Furthermore the same person had made his father wait for communion until his 'betters' had been served. Arch saw through this scheme of organized charity and condemned it in forthright terms. 'The curse of the Established Church', said R. A. Woods in 1891, 'is its country clergy, who are to a large extent aristocratic in their feeling and often exercise petty despotism over their parishes.' Saul Kane, the prize-fighting poacher in *The Everlasting Mercy*, spoke even stronger language. He told old 'purple parson':

> Your only fire's the jolly fire
> Where you can guzzle port with squire
> And back and praise his damned opinions
> About his temporal dominions.
> You let him give the man who digs,
> A filthy hut unfit for pigs,
> Without a well, without a drain,
> With mossy thatch that lets in rain,

> Without a 'lotment 'less he rent it
> And never meat, unless he scent it,
> But weekly doles of 'leven shilling
> To make a grown man strong and willing
> To do the hardest work on earth.
> But quite your damnest want of grace
> Is what you do to save your face;
> The way you sit astride the gates
> By padding wages out of rates;
> Your Christmas gifts of shoddy blankets
> That every working soul may thank its
> Loving parson, loving squire. . . .

The parson's reply succinctly summed up the attitude of the majority of Victorian country clergymen towards the social system existing in their villages:

> You think the Church an outworn fetter;
> Kane, keep it, till you've built a better.
> And keep the existing social state;
> I quite agree it's out of date,
> One does too much, another shirks,
> Unjust, I grant, but still . . . it works.

Today the position of the country clergy is very different from that of their Victorian predecessors. Their practical divorce from the land, since they have been deprived of their tithes and have probably sold their glebe, renders them less closely wedded to the status quo and has removed some part at least of their vested interest in the capitalist state. Hence there are undoubtedly more socialist and even communist-minded country parsons about than ever before in our history. Yet the clergy still remain conscious that every social change affects them for the worse. The abolition of coal royalties, the reduction of the interest on local loans, the nationalization of the railways, and the steady rise in national insurance contributions all hit the parson hard. They see the conventional church-going habits of the past being steadily undermined by the expanding prosperity and independence of the working classes; while a corresponding loosening of nineteenth-century conventions and moral restraints carries with it an implied, and sometimes outspoken, condemnation of Anglicanism as the out-dated guardian of Victorian prudery and inhibitions.

Money, from the parson's point of view, is nowadays getting into the wrong hands. The classes that mainly supported the Church financially in the past are growing steadily poorer; whilst the working man, who is becoming ever more prosperous, has no tradition of giving behind him. He is and always has been simply concerned with getting. Inflation, too, that is rapidly reducing the social status of the parson, can all too easily be attributed to unreasonable wage-demands. Hence, despite the noisy support given by a minority of country clergy to the left wing in politics and social movements, the harassed but mainly inarticulate majority continue to think and vote conservative, although Conservative Governments are not always their best friends. It is a question of putting up with the devil you know, rather than risk being swept away altogether by the winds of change.

CHAPTER IV

# Scholar and Man of Culture

THE QUIET, LEISURE, and beauty provided by the country rectory have frequently borne fruit in producing the poet, the scholar, and the man of letters; but they have also helped to secure for the countryside itself tiny oases of rich culture and courtly manners, whose influence has slowly but surely permeated the rural parishes. Even in the very worst periods of ignorance and neglect the parson has always been at least a semi-educated man, something that could not invariably have been said of the squire or the lord of the manor. Not uncommonly—almost invariably during the eighteenth and nineteenth centuries—the parson was a university graduate with an intellect aroused and stimulated by the scholars he had met there, and by the learned society in which he moved. Returning, as like as not, from these rarefied heights to the familiar but dull life of his native heath as the rector of his own or another's family living, he found himself cut off for the greater part of each year from the converse of his equals, and forced back upon the company of a bucolic squire or a pedantic village schoolmaster. Hence, not unnaturally, he sought other outlets for his mental powers. These he might find in academic study; in the cultivation and pursuit of brain-stimulating hobbies and amusing inventions; in the education of the members of his own family; and even by coaching gratuitously the bright village lad in whom he saw the germs of future brilliance. It is, in fact, no coincidence that the country parsonage has turned out so many able men and women in every walk of life.

One of the great literary figures of the medieval period was the author who, dreaming on the Malvern hills, saw the *Vision of Piers Plowman*. His name was William Langland, a bondsman who had been freed by taking the lower clerical orders in 1348. There is no record that he ever acquired a benefice, and eventually he drifted to London. None the less we are entitled to claim the great poem of this Broad Churchman as the work of a country clergyman. 'This Plowman', wrote Professor Coulton, 'stands for Humanity at its simplest and truest and highest; that is, for the human nature of Jesus Christ.' Langland was a lover of the beautiful, a close observer of Nature, a knowledgeable and indeed even a learned man. His

SCHOLAR AND MAN OF CULTURE

message can be summed up in the words: 'Do Well, Do Better, Do Best'; and, 'Chastity without Charity shall be chained in Hell'.

In his rural retreat of Lutterworth Rectory John Wyclif, aided by friends and admirers, produced the first Bible in English; and launched the Lollard Movement in the very teeth of the Official Church. At the country rectory of Bourne near Canterbury the judicious Richard Hooker perfected his *Ecclesiastical Polity* that cemented the foundations of Anglicanism as they had emerged from the Elizabethan Settlement. In the Wiltshire parsonage of Bemerton near Salisbury George Herbert drew his famous picture of the ideal country priest; while in the Lincolnshire rectory of Epworth the scholarship of Samuel and the sterling character of Susannah Wesley sowed the seeds of the Methodist Movement. The Oxford Movement owed much to Henry Newman's writings at Littlemore. And at Hursley John Keble put the Tractarian teaching to the test of practical pastoralia. Christian socialism was deeply indebted to Charles Kingsley's ministry in Eversley, where he composed his socialist novels and pamphlets, and tried out his Christian Chartism. These few outstanding examples provide ample illustration of the undoubted fact that the country parish and the country priest have produced the literary seed-beds out of which have sprung some of the greatest, most successful, and lasting influences, movements, and reforms within the Church. It is, one supposes, a commonplace to speak of the standard works that all down the centuries have poured out of the country parsonage. Of the great historians and antiquaries there is the seventeenth-century Tom Fuller working on the *History of the Church in Britain* at his cottage vicarage of Broadwindsor, and on the *Worthies of England* at Waltham Cross; or his younger contemporary, White Kennett, the father of local history, compiling his *Parish Antiquities* at Ambrosden. Then, in the early eighteenth century, Joseph Bingham wrote his *Origines Ecclesiastiae* while at Headbourne Worthy near Winchester from 1708 to 1722. The following century was even richer in historians from country parsonages: Connop Thirlwall at Kirby Underdale, Mandell Creighton at Embleton, R. W. Dixon at Warkworth, and J. H. Overton at Epworth, to name only four country parsons who made ample use of their leisured peace in painstaking historical research. Neither should that fine antiquary, local historian, and beloved parish priest, J. C. Atkinson, Rector of Danby in Cleveland from 1847 to 1900, be forgotten; he immortalized himself in a notable autobiography: *Forty Years in a Moreland Parish*. Henry Longden at Heyford in Northamptonshire carried on the tradition of the country clerical historian well into the middle of the twentieth century.

Of the scientists the country Church can claim men of the calibre

of Stephen Hales, perpetual curate of Teddington in Middlesex from
1709 to 1761, the physiologist and inventor, who wrote *Vegetable
Staticks* and *Statical Essays* on plant and animal physiology; and
invented artificial ventilators. Another inventor was Edmund Cartwright, Rector of Goadby Marwood in Leicestershire from 1779 to
1802, who revolutionized the weaving industry by creating the
power-loom, for which service to the community the House of
Commons voted him in 1809 the sum of £10,000. Later he experimented with agricultural processes on the estates of the Duke of
Bedford, particularly at Woburn Abbey. Another well-known
scientific country parson was J. S. Henslow of Hitcham. Henslow
was certainly an all-rounder. Botanist, geologist, chemist, ento-
mologist, conchologist, and archaeologist, he wrote many scientific
treatises, was the joint author of a standard work on the flora of
Suffolk, and invented some artificial fertilizers that Ipswich still
manufactures. He combined the post of Professor of Mineralogy
and Botany at Cambridge with his country rectory; but refused
that of naturalist on board *The Beagle*, during its five years'
voyage of exploration. Instead, on Henslow's advice, this important
job was offered to Charles Darwin, with whom the Rector ever
afterwards kept up a regular correspondence.

From the scientists we pass to the naturalists proper, headed, of
course, by Gilbert White of Selborne in Hampshire, whose *Natural
History and Antiquities* is the only work in English on natural
history that has attained the rank of a classic. White was an indefatigable traveller on horse-back through the southern half of
England, making careful notes of all he saw and heard. 'There is', he
wrote, 'a wonderful spirit of sociality in the brute creation, independent of sexual attachment: the congregation of gregarious birds in
the winter is a remarkable instance.' An ancestor of Gilbert's,
Charles Butler, the Laudian incumbent of Wotton St Lawrence in
Hampshire, was also a clerical naturalist. Speaking of his modest
benefice, a friend declared: 'A poor Vicarage, God wot for so worthy
a scholar'. Butler, too, was an all-rounder. A musician, who compiled *The Principles of Music*; a grammarian, whose *English Grammar* was praised by Dr Johnson himself; and above all a bee lover.
His magnum opus on this last subject was entitled: *De Feminin
Monarki or the Histori of Bees, shewing their admirable Nature and
Properties, their generation and Colonis; Their Government loyalti,
Art, Industri, Enimis, Wars, Maganimiti together with the right
ordering of them from tim' to tim'; and the sweet profit arising ther' of.*
He had previously experimented with silk worms and lost money;
but with his bees made large profits, and gave a marriage portion of
£400 to his daughter, whom he nicknamed 'his sweet honey girl'.

She married the Reverend R. White and became the great-grand-mother of Gilbert White. Charles Butler, who has been called the Father of English Bee-keeping, was the first to discover that bees are ruled over by a queen, and that the drones are male. Yet astonishingly enough he never realized that the queen and not the worker-bees was the mother of the swarm. He thought of her as a ruler, not as a slave who would one day be heartlessly discarded. However, he learnt that two queens cannot live together in one hive; and that in uniting two weak swarms—swarming was necessary in Butler's day to increase the numbers—one queen must first be killed. Bee-keeping proved a musical and poetic as well as a profit-able pastime. Listening to the bees preparing to swarm, the Vicar wrote:

> Hark, hark, methinks I hear in notes of choice
> This fairest lady's sweetest mournful voice.

He likewise made use of this hobby for sermonizing; and warned the more slovenly, dirty, and impure among his parishioners that the sensitive bees would sting them. 'Thou must not come among them smelling of sweat', he said, 'or having a stinking breath, caused either through the eating of leeks, onions or garlic, thou must not come puffing and blowing unto them, nor violently defend thyself when they seem to threaten thee, but softly moving thy hand before the face, gently put them by. In a word thou must be chaste, cleanly, sweet, sober, quiet and familiar. So will they love thee and know thee from all other.'

John Mossop, Rector of Covenham St Bartholomew in Lincoln-shire from 1830 to 1873, was an eminent ornithologist, who pub-lished *A Synopsis of British Land Birds* in 1841. He formed a museum of stuffed native birds, most of which he had shot himself. But he and his wife were also bird-watchers, watching and recording their habits; while Mrs Mossop kept a variety of pets. The Rector was something of a poet, who thus described the singing of a missel thrush on New Year's Day:

> One new year's morn, by Luda's favourite side,
> 'Twas sabbath morn to rest and praise allied—
> Where leads the path to Covenham's sacred pile,
> I heard the matin song and thought the while,
> O that man's voice would grateful swell, like thine,
> To hymn the praises of the Hand Divine.

Mossop was undoubtedly one of the pioneers of British ornithology, who had published his book before the giants, Yarrell, Morris, McGillivray, and others, had begun their work.

Another naturalist country parson was the Revd Octavius Pickard-Cambridge, Squarson of Bloxworth in Dorset, where he was Rector from 1848 to 1917. Pickard-Cambridge interested himself in every form of natural life; but his particular hobby was spiders, and between 1879 and 1881 he published his two-volume standard work on the *Spiders of Dorset*. His son later wrote of him: 'His was a good life to look back upon—full of the most varied interests, in natural history, in music, in gardening, in antiquities, in politics, as well as in his work as a clergyman. Until the last year or two of his life, he never seemed to grow old in mind, but remained, as ever, enthusiastic, warm-hearted, outspoken, full of fun and life, delighting in sharing his fun with others, and always ready to help or give pleasure to anyone in any matter.' Pickard-Cambridge was a Fellow of the Royal Society, a friend of Darwin, and an enthusiastic supporter of the theory of evolution.

To turn now to the Arts: The names of clerical novelists are legion, ranging from Laurence Sterne's *Tristram Shandy*, to the thirty romances of Sabine Baring-Gould, the socialist novels of Charles Kingsley, and the detective stories of the Revd J. Edmond Long, Rector of White Roothing in Essex for thirty-two years, who died in 1945. Long placed a notice at the end of his drive warning would-be visitors that he did not wish to enlarge the circle of his acquaintances, and bidding them beware of the dog.

The poets were equally numerous and varied. Clerical hymn writers, both Catholic and Evangelical, immediately leap to one's mind and include such famous country parsons as George Herbert, John Newton, J. M. Neale, Sabine Baring-Gould, and Henry Lyte. In contrast, there is the semi-pagan Robert Herrick with his fauns and satyrs and love lyrics; the realistic descriptions of social life by George Crabbe; and the ballad writers like R. S. Hawker, the singer of Trelawney and the Sangraal, whose immortal *Cornish Ballads* have firmly established his claim to be the English poet of the West. The Revd R. H. Barham was presented in 1814 to the livings of Snargate and Warehorne in Romney Marsh, where his church became a depôt for smugglers. On one occasion a large seizure of tobacco was made in Snargate belfry, while a keg of hollands was found under the vestry table! In this wild place 'Thomas Ingoldsby' collected much of his material for the famous *Legends*. Neither must we forget those poets like Francis Kilvert of Clyro who expressed themselves in prose.

On Easter Saturday, 16 April 1870, Kilvert recorded in his diary: 'I awoke at 4.30 and there was a glorious sight in the sky, one of the grand spectacles of the Universe. There was not a cloud in the deep wonderful blue of the heavens. Along the Eastern horizon there was a clear deep intense glow neither scarlet nor crimson but a mixture of both. This red glow was very narrow, almost like a riband and it suddenly shaded off into the deep blue. Opposite in the west the full moon shining in all its brilliance was setting upon the hill beyond the church steeple. Thus the glow in the east bathed the church in a warm rich tinted light, while the moon from the west was casting strong shadows. The moon dropped quickly down behind the hill bright to the last, till only her rim could be seen sparkling among the tops of the orchards on the hill. The sun rose quickly and his rays struck red upon the white walls of Penllan, but not so brilliantly as in the winter sunrisings.'

During the nineteenth century, as the *Dictionary of National Biography* bears faithful witness, the country clergy excelled themselves in the realm of scholarship and letters. Taking, for example, a single county at random in the eighteen-eighties, we find the following Lincolnshire scholars were then at work: the Church historians, G. G. Perry of Waddington and J. H. Overton of Epworth; the mathematicians, John Bond of Anderby and Francis Bashford of Minting; the antiquaries, Bishop Trollope of Leasingham, W. O. Massingberd of Ormsby, Canon Lodge of Scrivelsby, and H. J. Cheales of Friskney; the musicians, T. W. Sale of Halton Holgate and Thomas Barker of Revesby; the classical scholar, James Hildyard of Ingoldsby; and the artist, C. P. Terrott of Wispington. Men of much general learning included R. H. Charters of Kirton-in-Lindsay, Bartholomew Blenkiron of Little Cotes and A. E. More of Messingham. The Lincolnshire country parsons who worked with their hands were equally noteworthy; and in particular the skill of the woodcarver, T. J. M. Townsend, and the clock-maker, F. H. Sutton of Brant. The encyclopaedic knowledge and interests of some rural incumbents were, indeed, phenomenal. Edward Moore of Spalding was described as 'an authority upon matters of theology, politics, finance, poor-law, drainage, architecture, antiquities, agriculture, charity-management and education'.

An even better-known figure is Sabine Baring-Gould of Lew Trenchard in Devon, where he was the black squire for forty-three years. Baring-Gould was the author of a number of very popular hymns that included *Onward Christian Soldiers, Through the Night of Doubt and Sorrow,* and *On The Resurrection Morning.* He produced a prodigious output of popular religious and historical works, of which the *Lives of the Saints,* a vast hagiography in sixteen volumes compiled between 1872 and 1877 and written very largely in the interests of the Tractarian Movement, is probably the best known. Books on folk-lore like *Old Country Life* and *Old Fairy Tales Re-told,* and some thirty novels, which had a considerable

vogue in his life-time and created his literary reputation, but are
rarely read today, poured from his pen. In 1895 he published his
famous collection of English folk songs under the title of *Songs of
the West*, after more than a decade of research. He also wrote
numerous topographical, autobiographical, and archaeological
works, most of them notoriously inaccurate in detail; besides collecting stories of eccentric characters under their respective counties.
In all he produced some one hundred and thirty books, which were
accepted by some of the chief publishing houses in the land; and
were written over a period of seventy years from 1851 to 1921. 'He
was a giant in energy and literary appetite', declared his latest bio-
grapher. 'He was also an indifferent giant shewing no interest in
what others were doing.' Sabine Baring-Gould stood at his desk in
his lovely library at Lew Trenchard manor house writing because
he could not help writing; but he was not interested in reputation or
advancement, and remained unrecognized all through his life by the
Church he served. Nevertheless he was honoured and rewarded in
his old age by Clare College with an honorary fellowship, which he
greatly valued. So prodigious was his output that occasionally the
question was asked as to whether or no he employed a 'ghost'.
Baring-Gould did not deign to reply; but there is little doubt that he
wrote all his books himself.

The successful scholar, who graced a country parsonage, has been
remembered and honoured by posterity; while his less fortunate
brother has been completely forgotten, or at best is recalled today
for some work that he himself would not have considered either
valuable or important. John Skinner, for example, the unlucky
Rector of Camerton in Somerset, who committed suicide in 1831, is
ranked among the clerical diarists; and the voluminous manuscript
on the *History of Roman Remains in Britain*, that had occupied
most of his leisure hours during his life-time, still lies unread and
unpublished in the British Museum. Francis Goddard, who became
perpetual curate of Alderton, Wiltshire, in 1849, wrote in his
*Reminiscences*: 'Luckington is near Alderton and here dwelt one
Thomas Teasdale, curate for a good many years, breeding up a
family of five children on £80 per annum. He was a very learned
man, a great Greek scholar, engaged in making a lexicon for ten
years, when Liddell and Scott published their Lexicon and forever
destroyed poor Teasdale's chance of any benefit from his long years
of literary toil. After the death of his Rector, Mr Birch, of Easton
Grey, Mr Teasdale removed to Hullavington, where he gradually
in extreme penury wasted away.'

Many country parsons, who never actually wrote or published
anything themselves, were yet able to impart their considerable

scholarship to others: to the members of their own families, to the pupils they took in, or to some of the villagers in their parishes. An Oxford or Cambridge Don, who on marriage or for other reasons was presented by his College to one of their country livings, often brought to his rustic retirement a high standard of culture and good manners that greatly benefited the countryside. Men of the type of William Sampson, the seventeenth-century Rector of Clayworth in Nottinghamshire, William Cole and James Woodeforde in the eighteenth century, or James Lee Warner in the nineteenth, certainly did very well in their villages, where their parishioners grew to love and respect them. From this type of literary household great literary figures have emerged, such as Jane Austen from Steventon, Samuel Butler from Languar, Lord Tennyson from Somersby, and the Brontë sisters of Haworth, to name a few at random. Matthew Arnold, too, was the indirect product of a similar parsonage; since his mother was Mary Penrose. Let us take a look at the Reverend John Penrose's Vicarage of Fledborough in Nottinghamshire in the year of Waterloo, through the medium of the family journal: There is the whole family—at least father, mother, and the four daughters, for the two scholarly sons, John and Tom, are away in Oxford—on a winter's evening, when the parish work is done, seated round the candle-lit parlour table: reading their books, writing their letters, learning their languages, and even tackling their mathematics. 'We have', said Mrs Penrose enthusiastically, 'French, Italian, History, Divinity, Biography, Arithmetic, Penmanship, Needlework, and to crown all Mathematics; for Euclid is begun again and proceeded on with redoubled alacrity.' 'I assure you', a friend wrote of them, 'that when they are all seated round the table after tea, when Mr Penrose used to read the *Life of Sir Thomas More* I never saw a more delightful scene.' Neither must it be forgotten that Edmund Cartwright's daughter, Elizabeth, the future authoress of *Mrs Markham's History of England*, married into the Penrose family.

One valuable contribution from the country rectory that has been seeing the light of day in modern times, is the personal diary, register, journal, or commonplace book, kept by a large number of country clergy from the sixteenth century onwards, with no idea of publication, but purely for their own amusement, convenience, and information. Many of these journals naturally make dull reading yet even the dullest is of interest when it is more than a hundred years old; and some are of high literary quality, notably that of Francis Kilvert of Clyro. Others are mere jottings. The Elizabethan Robert Leband of Rolleston, Notts., a scholar and shrewd observer of his fellow men and women, although himself of humble birth, 'made a confidant of his register book'. Against the entry of name and date he would add a pithy comment of his own; discreetly turning it into Latin if unfavourable and therefore not to be repeated in the village by the parish clerk. Here is an example: 'Christopher Bettisome about three score years of age a man of low stature, a painful workman in ditchyinge and mowinge, but being in his last years weake through sickness he was the townes neat heard until his death was buryed on Wednesday the fourth of November (1590).' But of William Forrest, who died in the following year at the age of sixty, he wrote very differently in Latin: 'A cunning fellow, I will not say crafty, of little faith or hope of eternal life, if it is permissible to regard words as an index to the mind.'

Giles Moore, the seventeenth-century Rector of Horsted Keynes in Sussex, on the other hand, was more interested in his accounts than his fellow creatures. He headed his journal with the words: 'Wee reckon our expenses but not our sins; wee account what wee expend but not where wee offend'; and provided us with some illuminating seventeenth-century prices. For instance, six weeks board and lodging in London, in comparative comfort, cost as little as £1 10s. 0d., but a single 'shaggy demi castor hat' fetched 16s. 6d. The best known and perhaps the most readable of all country diaries is that of James Woodeforde, Fellow of New College, Oxford, and Rector of Weston Longueville near Norwich from 1776 to 1802. It revealed a latitudinarian country-gentleman-parson, who was more interested in his meals, his games of cards, his coursing of hares, his visits to Norwich and the West country than in his religious duties as a clergyman. At the same time he was a generous, kindly man, who lived on the very best terms with his squire and parishioners, to the last of whom he was all too willing to act the Good Samaritan.

Earlier diaries culled from the late sixteenth and seventeenth centuries disclose the inner working of the Puritan mind and spirit, as seen for example in the journals and autobiographies of ministers like Ralph Josselin of Earls Colne in Essex, Henry Newcome of Manchester, and Richard Baxter of Kidderminster. Josselin, a typical Puritan, combined thrift with piety. A staunch supporter of Parliament, he yet deplored the execution of Charles I, and had little sympathy with the fanaticism and extravagances of such sects as the Quakers. 'Sad are the fits at Coxall [Coggeshall]', he remarked wryly, 'like the pow-wowing among the Indies.' He strongly disliked the rule of Cromwell's Major-Generals; noted Oliver's own death with indifference; and warmly welcomed the return of Charles II. Josselin refused to join the ranks of the Bartholomew Martyrs; and so retained his living until his death in 1683. That living was a good one, being worth more than £80 per annum; and in various ways: by careful farming, legacies from relations, and the profits of schoolmastering, he gradually amassed a considerable fortune. Money-making did not, however, detract in the least from his devotional life or ministerial duties. He uttered no idle words when he declared: 'I hope the Lord will keepe my feete in uprightness that I may walke alwaies with him and I trust it shall bee my endeavour more than ever.'

Henry Newcome was a clergyman of the same kidney, although more deeply committed to the Presbyterian cause. He never received episcopal ordination and was eventually ejected from his curacy. Yet he, too, had deplored the King's murder, and rejoiced in the restoration of the Stuarts. Under the Commonwealth he had found himself a well-paid post in Manchester, worth £120 per annum, where he laboured mightily for the Lord. Here he suffered from the interference of some of the more fanatical sects. 'About this time [February 1652]', he wrote, 'the Lord gave me much success in my ministry, and there were many affected with the Word, and began to make a very hopeful profession, both in my own parish and in the neighbourhood of those that came to our congregation. But Satan envied us, and assaulted us very dangerously. The first assault was by the independents.'

Richard Baxter was another moderate Presbyterian, whose autobiography gives a pleasing picture of his ministry at Kidderminster. 'The congregation', he recorded, 'was usually full, so that we were fain to build five galleries after my coming thither, the most commodious and convenient that ever I was in. On the Lords-day there was no disorder to be seen in the streets, but you might hear an hundred families singing psalms and repeating sermons as you passed through the streets.'

A friend of Baxter's was John Wade, who served the curacy of Hammersmith for over forty years from 1662 until 1707. Wade, although a Presbyterian at heart as his recently discovered diary conclusively proves, remained uneasily within the Establishment. But his habit of constantly preaching against the profanation of the Sabbath and making use of extempore prayers in public worship, earned Bishop Henchman of London's stern reproof that he was 'not hearty to the liturgy and government established'. None the less he was a most conscientious and faithful parish priest, a scholar and writer of some note, and an extremely keen horticulturalist. This last hobby must, as in the case of the Elizabethan William Harrison of Radwinter, endear him to all garden lovers. Harrison had written of his garden: 'For mine own part, good reader, let me boast a little of my garden, which is small, and the whole Area thereof little above 300 foot of ground, such hath bene my good lucke in pur-

F

chase of the varietie of simples, that notwithstanding my small abilitie, there are verie neere three hundred of one sort and other conteined therein, no one of them being common or usuallie to bee had.' John Wade's garden was a much more lordly and luxurious one. His parsonage at Hammersmith was described in 1706 as a 'very handsome seat'. He possessed the best of everything then available in plants, trees, and bushes. In his orchard he grew apples, peaches, apricots, cherries, plums, nectarines, strawberries, rasp-berries, gooseberries, currants, and vines. In the kitchen garden he planted beans, lettuces, spinach, parsley, onions, horse-radishes, besides a well-stocked herbal plot; while his flower-beds contained roses, violets, auriculas, tulips, gillyflowers, jonquils, carnations, anemones, stocks, polyanthuses, oxlips, primroses, and hollyhocks. Wade did not grudge spending money on his garden; in fact in less than four months, from November 1672 until March 1673, he laid out the large sum, for those days, of £3 19s. 10d.

The eighteenth century was the age par excellence of the letter-writer, the journal-keeper, and the diarist. Apart from James Woodeforde himself there were several clerical diarists and letter-writers, who have achieved fame. These included Benjamin Rogers, the farmer-scholar of Carlton in Bedfordshire; William Cole of Bletchley, the antiquarian and friend of Horace Walpole; Patrick St Clair of Sustead, the agent of the Ashe-Windhams of Felbrigg in Norfolk; William Jones, the poor down-trodden curate-school-master of Broxbourne; and the morbidly introspective John Skinner, Rector of Camerton in Somerset. The Evangelical Revival towards the close of the century, which flourished in some country districts, likewise bore fruit in the keeping of personal records, although of a more devotional or missionary flavour.

Diary-keeping amongst the Victorian country clergy, judging from the large numbers that have survived, was an extremely popular pastime. Doubtless they felt an urge to record, if only for their own personal satisfaction or that of their families and descen-dants, the remarkable range of 'good works' now being carried out in the villages. These varied from the wholesale repair of the church, the building of a school, and the setting up of clubs, to the creation of a full scale community life in the parish. John Holdich, Rector of Bulwick from 1862 until 1892, bequeathed his journal to his suc-cessors in the hope it might inspire them to further efforts. 'When I began this Book', he declared, 'I intended leaving it to my succes-sors in the Rectory as . . . concerning the Parish, and therefore most interesting to whomsoever should be called to minister in this place.' And to this day a copy of the diary is to be found in the church safe.

Generally speaking the very earnestness and conscientious detail of such personal records made for lack of entertainment or publicity value; and this was especially true of those which were written while on holiday abroad. No country parson, apparently, could go abroad—and some of the richer ones spent considerable periods in each year away from their native land—without returning with full note-books of all that they had seen and heard of an edifying and educational nature. I still possess those of my great-grandfather, Edward Pearson, who was Rector of Springfield near Chelmsford for more than sixty years, and used to pass much of the winter in Italy, where he eased his conscience by occasionally instructing a child of some English resident for Confirmation or by performing some special duties. His closely written and extremely boring pages are, however, relieved and enlightened by illustrations in water colour.

Here and there, of course, we strike gold in the shape of remarkably interesting and highly entertaining reminiscences and autobiographies. Those of Sabine Baring-Gould have already been mentioned; but others are equally noteworthy: the adventures, for instance, of that robust evangelical Archdeacon Philpot, both in the Isle of Man and his native Norfolk; or the extremely readable autobiography of the aristocratic Edward Bligh. Possibly one of the most lively and outspoken was a slim volume that appeared in 1890 under the title of *My Rectors: by a Quondam Curate*.

Nothing is probably staler or more dry-as-dust than by-gone religious controversy; but it has none the less to be recorded that the country parsonage often proved a fruitful source and happy hunting-ground for such theological and doctrinal disputations. From this safe vantage point Puritan thundered against Anglican, High Church against Low Church, Latitudinarian against Non-Juror, Evangelical against Tractarian, and Anglo-Catholic against Modernist. Books, pamphlets, articles, and broadsheets have poured from the country parson's pen on these and kindred subjects. But rarely have they proved to be of lasting value or outstanding literary merit. Sometimes they have even caused strife and bickering in the parson's own family or parish. Samuel Wesley, a prominent whig controversialist, once left his wife Susannah for a whole year because she refused to accept William III as King of England. 'Sukey', he cried in wrath, 'if that be the case you and I must part; for if we have two Kings, we must have two beds.' Another whig controversialist, the latitudinarian White Kennett of Shottesbroke, found his squire, Francis Cherry, harbouring the non-juror Henry Dodwell, who in his turn was endeavouring to form a non-juring Cave of Abdullum in the village, and lure away into it the congregation from the parish church.

The writing and distribution of tracts, whether of a High, Low, or Broad Church complexion, was a favourite pastime with some country clergy. Benjamin Philpot, the fervent evangelical Rector of Great Cressingham, both composed his own and accepted for distribution those of others. Wherever he went he carried a number in his pocket, which he handed out on every possible occasion, particularly when there were any Roman Catholic priests around! One day he offered a booklet to a stranger, who promptly sat down and filled in the initials on the title page with his own name, for he was the author! Philpot later wrote in his journal: 'Horace is right. *Fronti nulla fides.*'

It cannot be denied that by and large the country parsonage has fathered a wealth of scholarship, erudition, and culture that has enriched our land with pure knowledge, new beauty, fresh invention, entertainment, and a continuous flow of men of learning and culture, who have helped to civilize the rude countryside as the makers of its manners as well as of its morals.

On the other hand it must be confessed that the scholar-parson has not invariably been a success in the country benefice. As an unkind critic once commented, he has sometimes the unfortunate habit of being incomprehensible on Sunday, and invisible for the rest of the week. P. H. Ditchfield in *Old-Time Parson* tells the delightful story of the learned Shropshire Rector, who used to take great folio volumes into the pulpit with him in order to prove some obscure theological point by quoting copiously from their pages. His congregation, composed entirely of illiterate rustics, grew restive under this treatment; and matters reached a head on one particularly dark and wintery afternoon. The sage, surrounded by candles and now well into his stride, looked as though he might continue to hold forth indefinitely; so one by one, under cover of the growing darkness, the yokels slipped away until only the parish clerk was left. He bore it as long as he could; but his patience was finally exhausted by some long quotations from St Augustine. He, therefore, boldly addressed the preacher: 'Sir, when you've done, p'r'aps you'll blow out the candles, lock the door, and put the key under the mat.' Canon Charles Smyth, speaking of the overall position of the scholar-parson, summed the matter up when he wrote in *Church and Parish*: 'For all priests, whether liberal or orthodox, the pastoral calling must be paramount. There is a place for scholars in the ministry: but, unless they are prepared like their less intellectually gifted brethren, to say their prayers and love their people, their orthodoxy or their liberalism will be sterile as regards the purpose for which they have been ordained.'

CHAPTER V

# Sportsman and Recreationalist

THE COUNTRY PRIEST in every age has taken full advantage of his
rural surroundings to shoot and trap for the pot, and to join in the
rustic pastimes and merry-making that helped to lighten his hard
manual labours and primitive living conditions. These recreations
have always been permissible. But when the parson took to hunting
and hawking, to drinking heavily in the tavern and gambling with
his parishioners, it was an altogether different story. The medieval
parish priest was sternly forbidden both by Canon Law and by his
Diocesan Superiors to indulge in any such activities. Nevertheless
he not infrequently succumbed to these temptations, which he
sought to disguise by changing into lay attire and donning a hood in
order to hide the tonsure. However, the conditions of medieval life
might well excuse much that today would be regarded as serious
moral offences and bring the clergy into considerable disrepute.
Drunkenness, for example, was for long regarded with an indulgent
eye. Water, of course, was often unfit to drink; and until modern
hygenic methods were introduced into the countryside the con-
sumption of some substitute such as ale, beer, or wine was essential.
These were intoxicants that could only too easily lead to intemperance. Possibly it was a priest who composed the medieval
bibulous song that begins:

'Tis my intention, gentle sir, to perish in a tavern.

Deprived of the comforts and joys of a normal home-life, and
unable to obtain or afford books, all too many country priests in the
Middle Ages spent their leisure hours in the village ale-house, where,
despite the wrath or exhortations of Bishop and Archdeacon, they
sought to drown their sorrows and forget their hardships in the arms
of Bacchus. A state of affairs, judging from visitation returns and the
records of archdeacons' courts, which certainly did not cease at the
Reformation. Puritans might thunder forth their denunciations
against the Romish, whore-mongering, drunken Anglican parson;
but disgraceful scenes like the following were still only too common:
'That about Midsomer last Mr Garth [Vicar of Charlton, Oxon.]
and this examinant did play together against William Witham and

85

Thomas Preist . . . att football att which tyme the said Mr Garth was overtaken with drinck that he did sometymes reele, and att that tyme one Mumford a cooper was wrastling there with another and afterwards lying along upon the ground on his back, the said Mr Garth uppon a wager then offered to be layd did attempt to take him upp. Where uppon the said Cooper catched hold of him that the sayd Mr Garth fell downe backward and thereby the sleeve of his Jerkin was torne.' John Blythe, Rector of Kirkheaton in York-shire, was in 1567 'so drunke that he could not take his service'. Parsonage ale-houses, railed at by medieval bishops, were still flourishing in the Elizabethan Age. In 1575 a number were un-earthed, notably at Adel, Whitkirk, Ilkley, and Kettlewell; while at Skipton it was reported: 'The Vicar's brother doth dwell with him in the vicaredge howse and sometymes breweth ale and selleth to his friends.'

During Elizabethan and Stuart times, until the Commonwealth put a stop to them, the principal means of raising funds in a parish was by way of Church Ales. For these the parson was chiefly responsible. When some heavy item of expenditure came along like the rebuilding of the church tower, the recasting of the bells, the raising of stock to set the poor to work, or the buying of a silver communion cup, a Church Ale was organized at Whitsuntide. Invitations were sent out to neighbouring parishes, and people came from far and near. The church bells were rung, and long tables were erected in the church itself, in the churchyard, or on the village green, where a gargantuan meal was served consisting of such substantial items as breasts of veal, quarters of lamb, and roast fowls, as well as eggs, cheese, fruit, butter, and spices. Great barrels of ale were broached and drunk, while minstrels played. Afterwards there were church plays, games, sports, and dancing; and, it must be admitted, often a good deal of drunkenness, rough horse-play, and disorderly conduct. 'Well is he', we are told, 'that can get the soonest to it, and spendes the most at it, he is counted the godliest man of all the rest . . . because it is spent upon his church for-sooth.' In such a competition the parson himself apparently was not backward; and during the Civil Wars and under the Common-wealth his promotion of and participation in these jollifications, was one of the charges brought against him in order to secure his convic-tion. Another charge, often linked with it, was drunkenness. It was said, for instance, of William Underwood, minister of Harby in Lincolnshire: 'Mr Underwood is very scandalous in his life and con-verssacion by his continual frequenting of Ailehouses and that some-times of the Sabboth dayes and keepinge Comapanie theire with men of ill faime, viz. Coblers and Pedlers and such as spend what

they gett in drinkinge and Tiplinge in Ailehouses and thereby has
made himselfe a skorne and derision to others in havinge the back-
side of his clothes besmered over with creame by those that keepe
him in Company.' Thomas Pickard, Rector of St Mary's Stamford,
was accused of being 'a frequenter of Innes and Ailehouses', and
'is oftentimes distempered with drinke and quarrelsome and apt to
abuse honest men and women with his tongue'; while the wretched
John Terry, curate of Smarden in Kent, was reported to have
become so drunk 'that he hath bene found lyinge in the streete and
dirt, not able to helpe himselfe'.

The eighteenth and early nineteenth centuries were the age of
heavy drinking par excellence; of four- or five-bottle men, who
consumed vast quantities of port and brandy. Neither was the
practice regarded as being unwholesome or discreditable as far as
the country clergy were concerned. When, indeed, a certain Bishop
rebuked one of his clergy for being drunk, the latter replied: 'But,
my lord, I was never drunk on duty.' 'On duty!' exclaimed the
bishop, 'when is a clergyman not on duty?' 'True', acknowledged
the other, 'I never thought of that.' John Wesley's mortal enemy,
George White, curate of Colne in Lancashire, eventually drank himself to death. We read of drunken parsons falling into the grave
themselves while conducting a funeral; of others who had to be
carried away from a visitation dinner by the Bishop's own servants;
and of Bishop Bloomfield of London suggesting to his Essex
incumbents that 'a good deal of port wine' was a sovereign remedy
for the ague. Methodists and Evangelicals conducted a vigorous
campaign against drunkenness that left a permanent impression
upon the Victorian country clergy, who proceeded to set up
branches of the Church of England Temperance Society and wage
war against excessive drinking in their villages. However, as the
nineteenth century wore on the developing Anglo-Catholic Movement had not the same sympathy with strait-laced Puritanism.
When staying at Malvern Richard Seymour 'heard a lecture from a
Mr Wright on a Model Parish, i.e. one in which no alcohol shall be
drunk'; and commented in his diary: 'His views, I thought, very
intemperate and quixotic.'

In private no doubt the majority of country parsons still enjoyed
their bottle of port or glass of brandy; and laid down plenty of good
wine in their cellars to mature in their old age or for their successors. But in public, at any rate, they found sobriety and even
abstemiousness coincided better with a growing popular opinion on
the right type of conduct to be pursued by a clerk in holy orders.
Allied with public opinion was the new law, the Clergy Discipline
Act, 55 and 56 Vict. C. 32, which included drunkenness among the

moral offences for which an incumbent could be deprived of his living. Gone, indeed, were the days when a drinking, swearing parson was treated by his parishioners with indulgence and even respect, as denoting that he was but human like themselves, with tastes and failings not dissimilar from their own. 'My good woman', a visitor once asked an old peasant in a wild Devonshire moorland parish, 'can you point out the Vicar of your parish?' 'Did 'ee see a man go by on a white horse?' 'I did.' 'An' was he blind drunk?' 'He certainly was rolling in the saddle.' 'And was he cursin' and swearin' fit to burn his tongue out?' 'He was using very shocking language.' 'Ah, then, that's our parson. An' a dear good man he be!' That type of story was now being replaced by this sort of thing: a Bishop decided to travel up to London third class. Opposite him in the carriage a miner scrutinized his person carefully; at last he said: 'Are you a curate?' 'I *was* once', replied the Bishop modestly. 'Ah', said the miner shaking his head sadly, 'drink, I suppose.' Such a prim and proper attitude, if carried to extremes, can defeat its professed object of raising the parson's prestige and popularity. 'William', exclaimed his vicar sternly, 'I am deeply grieved to see you in such a condition.' 'Were you ever tight, parson?' asked the drunk. 'I? Certainly not, never in all my life.' 'What a dull life you must have had', retorted the alcoholic as he turned and zig-zagged his way down the village street.

The drinking parson is often associated with the fighting parson, although the two do not necessarily go together; for there have always been plenty of pugnacious clergy about. In the rough and tumble of the medieval village the priest had to be prepared to defend himself with fist, club, or dagger as well as bell, book, and candle; and it is scarcely surprising to find sixteenth- and seventeenth-century visitation returns full of references to brawls involving country clergy. Melchior Smith, vicar of Hessle near Hull, went into his church on All Saints' Eve 1564 and pulled Nicholas Laborn, a seaman, by the beard. 'And also gave him such a strooke upon the face with his fist that Laborn brast out of bloode boothe at the mouth and at the nose.' At Towersey in Buckinghamshire during the year 1607 the churchwardens presented their minister, Richard Jones, as being 'both a quarreler, a fighter, and a drunkard in public places'. Some thirty years later the curate of Smarden in Kent was described in even more outspoken terms: 'Mr Terry', it was asserted, 'is a fighter and that not only in his owne house but a breaker of the King's peace, in strikinge others, both men and women, and that even at the church door.' Such stories were certainly not uncommon, nor unproven in Elizabethan and Stuart times; and during the Civil Wars some parsons put their fighting

Cyril Pearson, Rector of Springfield, Essex, 1886–96, a famous chess and croquet player.

Horace Fuller Rackham, Vicar of High Wych 1886–1928.

DR SYNTAX TAKING POSSESSION OF HIS LIVING.

DR SYNTAX READING HIS TOUR.

Illustrations by Rowlandson for William Combe's *The Tour*

A NOBLE HUNTING PARTY.

THE HARVEST HOME.

of Dr Syntax, 1812. (By courtesy of the British Museum.)

The Vicar of the parish receiving his tithes.

prowess to very good use in the service of the King. The most
notorious was probably Michael Hudson, Rector of Uffington, who
fell in defence of Woodford House in Lincolnshire, which he and a
party of cavaliers had seized in 1648 and held against the Roundheads. 'Hudson', declared Bishop Kenneth, 'fought his way up to
the leads; and when he saw they were pushing in upon him, threw
himself over the battlements [another account says he caught hold
of a spout or outstone], and hung by the hands as intending to fall
into the moat beneath, till they cut off his wrists and let him drop,
and then ran down to hunt him in the water, where they found him
paddling with his stumps, and barbarously knocked him on the
head.' Another royalist country parson, Thomas Jones of Offwell
in Devonshire, was the reputed cause of Waller's defeat at Devizes;
for which Oxford awarded him the D.D.

Henry Greathead of Granby, Notts., defending himself against
alleged scandals, wrote to the Archbishop of York on 25 May 1698:
'And as for fighting I must truly own I have been guilty of it but not
within the last twelve months last past and am at this present under
a solemn obligation to several Gentlemen never to strike any man
again unless to vindicate myself from the assaults of Highwaymen.'
In the alehouse at Langar in the same county on 20 January 1707,
two clergymen came to blows after a heated theological argument.
One of them, the Reverend W. Selby of Elton, had his cravat pulled
off and was thrown violently to the ground.

A favourite victim of the eighteenth-century fighting parson was,
of course, the Methodist. George White used to muster his toughs
by beat of drum and lead them in person to the beating up of unfortunate Wesleyan congregations. W. M. Thackeray in *Vanity Fair*
has drawn a vivid picture of the pugilist Rector at the time of Waterloo in the person of Bute Crawley, Rector of Queen's Crawley:
'At College he pulled stroke-oar in the Christchurch boat, and had
thrashed all the best bruisers of the "town". He carried his taste for
boxing and athletic exercises into private life: there was not a fight
within twenty miles at which he was not present.' Boxing, we
note, under the Marquess of Queensberry's rules, had taken the
place of unscientific fighting; and the Victorian parson, who was
usually a gentleman, no longer engaged in the latter type of undig-
nified scrimage. There were, of course, exceptions; notably the
famous clerical bruiser, Jack Hannaford, the friend and boon companion of Parson Froude. There was, too, the celebrated battle of
Royd Lane narrated by Charlotte Brontë in *Shirley*, where the
united Sunday Schools of the parishes of Whinbury, Nunnely, and
Briarfield, led by their three Rectors, won a signal victory over the
unholy alliance of the Dissenting and Methodist Schools. But on the

whole the Arnold tradition of muscular Christianity, that the parson had learnt at his public school, was used solely in the interests of justice, humanity, and chivalry. The Victorian fighting clergyman, in fact, was the kind of man who would knock down a brute mercilessly thrashing a horse, defend a lady against the unwelcome attentions of a sinister villain, or courageously grapple with a burglar caught red-handed stealing the family silver. He could also protect himself effectively against an unprovoked assault. A curate visiting one of the less desirable homes in his parish suddenly found himself facing a shut-door, an ox of a man, and a demand to hand over his gold watch. As it happened this particular cleric had won his boxing blue at Cambridge; and he later had occasion to visit his would-be assailant several times in hospital. Today the country priest rarely has any reason for using his fists, except possibly in a boxing-ring at the local scout hut; but the knowledge that he can still do so effectively is often a matter of pride to his parishioners.

To the Puritan and the Evangelical another of the deadlier sins was dancing. No doubt the medieval priest danced quite a lot: round the May-pole with his habit flying about his ears, at marriage feasts, and even in the church itself, although Canon law explicitly forbade any cleric to dance no matter what his excuse might be. Dancing, indeed, was regarded as sinful, since not only was it pre-Christian in origin, but often most un-Christian in its practical manifestations. Particularly reprehensible was the parson who was caught dancing in the tavern; and in this matter the Reformed Church was if anything stricter than its Medieval predecessor. It was said, for example, of Tristram Tildesley, minister of Rufford and Marstone in Queen Elizabeth's reign, that 'not having the fear of God before his eyes very unmodestlye and to the great sclaunder of the ministerye . . . upon Sondaies or hollidaies hath daunced emongest light and youthful companie both men and women at weddings and rishbearings . . . in the parishe of Rufford and the parishe of Marstone and other parishes therabouts and espediallie upon one Sonday or holidaie . . . in his dancing or after wantonlye and dissolutelye he kissed a mayd or yong woman then a dauncer in his companie, wherat divers persons were offended and so sore greved that ther was wepons drawn and great dissention arose or was lyke to aryse therupon to the great disquietnes of God's peace and the Quenes Majesty.' None the less, despite puritanical frowns and the protests of Mrs Grundy, the country parson continued to dance when and where he could, and permitted his wife to engage in the same pastime. William Lynche, Rector of Beauchamp Roothing in Essex, was examined before the Archdeacon's court in 1563 for allowing his wife to dance at the common alehouse, where she had certainly misbehaved herself 'with bachelors and willd youth'.

Dancing, which was suppressed under the Commonwealth and Protectorate, was revived after the Restoration; and the eighteenth-century latitudinarian parson had few qualms about indulging in this pleasant recreation. However, in certain quarters it was still considered unbecoming in a clergyman to dance. An advertisement in the *Reading Mercury* of 1726 ran as follows: 'A curate wanted, who will have easy duty and a stipend of £50 per annum, besides valuable perquisites. He must be zealously affected to the present Government and never forsake his principles, regular in his morals, sober and abstemious, grave in his dress and deportment, choice in his company, and exemplary in his conversation. He must be of superior abilities, studious, and careful in his employment of time, a lover of fiddling but no dancer.' Gradually the prickings of the Evangelical Conscience began to influence the behaviour of many of the clergy. On 11 January 1832, the young curate of Havant near Portsmouth, Richard Seymour, drove his two sisters out to a children's dance at Codlington. 'My conscience not at ease', he recorded afterwards in his diary, 'Doubtful therefore whether I should have been there. I feel a great and I hope proper fear of being thought not to live up to what I preach. Shall avoid such things in future. May God mercifully guide me in my participation of those things which are perhaps lawful but not expedient.' To this day that great evangelical society, the Church Pastoral Aid Society, will only make grants towards a curate's stipend to those parishes which agree to eschew dancing and cards as forms of parochial amusement or for money-making purposes.

In later life Seymour as Rector of Kinwarton became a staunch adherent of the Catholic Revival; and his views on dancing underwent a change. He thus described the first of his harvest teas in 1851: 'Nearly all the parish were there sooner or later. All above 13 years old paid 6d each, and money was collected to help it. Children paid nothing. There was abundance of tea, bread and cake. We had three musicians, and at 7 the people began to dance which continued till 10.30 when we sang "God save the Queen" and dispersed. It has been a most successful feast. All seemed satisfied, especially the dancers. And the cost was very trifling.' Broad churchmen also approved of dancing. F. W. Tuckwell of Stockton organized concerts and dances in the winter for his young people. The latter were especially popular. 'Tell 'ee, Parson', one yokel confided to him, 'this be better foon than getting toight.' In the summer they were continued on the Rectory lawn; while dancing classes were arranged for the lads who wished to learn. Today dancing is probably the principal form of youthful recreation in the villages; and some parish priests have even been known to rock 'n roll themselves in their cassocks!

The hunting parson has rarely been a popular figure. The Church Authorities have usually frowned upon him, and the puritanical layman has raised his hands in horror. On the other hand he often endeared himself to a lot of people who were not normally very 'churchy'. Generally speaking it would be true to say that he hunted simply because he liked it; but in his palmiest days there were possibly some clergymen who did so from a sense of snob-values, or even as part of their clerical duties. Charles Kingsley at Eversley for example, hunted in the interests of muscular Christianity.

Hunting parsons were not uncommon in the Middle Ages; for we find William Langland condemning them root and branch in his *Vision of Piers Plowman*:

Haukying other hontying, yf eny of hem vsie
Shal lese ther-fore hus lyue-lode, and hus life parauenture:

In the Elizabethan Age they were no more popular. The Rectors of Patrington in Yorkshire, and Coddington in Cheshire were notable huntsmen. But their churchwardens, who 'hold it offensive', presented them to the Archdeacon. An Essex clergyman in 1610 arrived late at his church one Sunday morning on horseback; and being asked by his wardens whether he intended to take the service and preach, replied: 'So God should judge his soule, he muste and would go seeke his dogge which . . . was stolne, which he would not loose for a sermon.' One of the charges brought against the Vicar of Somerby in Leicestershire, which led to the subsequent sequestration of his living during the Civil Wars, was that he 'did ride on huntinge in his perambulation after a hare, in his surplice, and leapt over a gate and so teare his surplice, that the parish was inforced to provide a new surplice for him to read prayers in, and to keepe the old one for him to hunt in.'

But by the following century the hunting parson had become a fairly respectable person; and many pursued this form of sport, together with its corollary of shooting game, only too zealously. Advertisements like the following began to appear in the newspapers: 'To be sold by Auction by Hoggart & Phillips, Old Broad Street, London, the next presentation to a most valuable living in one of the finest sporting counties.' 'What a pity', wrote William Jones, the knowledgeable curate of Broxbourne, 'that so many of these drones are admitted into the Church . . . keen sportsmen, sharp shooters and mighty hunting Nimrods of the cloth, as it is called by way of eminence. For the accommodation of the latter class of these Reverends daily advertisements appear for the sale of the next presentation of valuable livings, rendered much more valuable, as being "situated in fine sporting countries", "plenty of game", "a pack of staunch fox-hounds kept in the neighbourhood".' The Reverend W. B. Daniel was a parson of this type, who devoted his entire life to the pursuit of hunting, shooting, coursing, and fishing; and published a widely acclaimed book on the subject entitled *Rural Sports*. He took a particular interest in the old controversy concerning the inter-breeding of dogs and foxes, believing it to be true. He lived to be over eighty; and towards the end of his life his conscience apparently became uneasy. Was it right for a priest in the Church of England to devote so much of his time to catching birds, animals, or fish, and so little to converting men, women, and children? He had, indeed, been a better keeper of dogs than a shepherd of souls, and had fished for salmon and trout rather than his fellow creatures. So he decided to make amends; and in 1822 another book appeared from his pen: *Plain thoughts . . . Upon the Lord's Prayer*.

As the nineteenth century wore on into the Victorian Age the attitude of the country clergy towards blood sports slowly changed; and they thought twice before engaging in pastimes that a few decades previously they would have taken as a matter of course. Sydney Smith wrote from his Yorkshire Rectory of Foston-le-Clay to Lady Holland: 'I have laid down two rules for the country: first, not to smite the partridge. . . . If anything ever endangers the Church it will be the strong propensity to shooting for which the clergy are remarkable.' Francis Goddard likewise recorded in his *Reminiscences*: 'I had been in the habit of riding to hounds before I was in Holy Orders, and I continued to hunt during the time I was in Winterbourne Basset nor did my parishioners seem to object to the practice. But as aforesaid it was a waning practice. As a rule those clergy that rode to hounds rode forward. After I left Winterbourne Basset I never hunted.' The leaven of the Evangelical Revival was at work. However, in the West Country and East Anglia hunting clergy were still very much alive. Bishop Henry Phillpotts of Exeter had a good deal of trouble with men like the notorious Vicar of Knowstone, Parson Froude. A. G. Bradley, while a boy in the 'sixties, described such a character whom he chanced to meet at a rectory luncheon party on Exmoor. 'He looked as nearly like a stud-groom as was possible for a man clad in expensive raiment. He had a bullet head of rather short-cropped hair, a heavy, dull face, clean-shaved but for a strip of coachman's whisker beside his ear, and a monocle screwed into one eye. He wore a pepper-and-salt suit of rather sporting cut and a white scarf with a fox-head pin in it.' At that date there were no less than twenty Devonshire parsons keeping packs of hounds, of whom the celebrated Jack Russell of Swymbridge was one, and the number of black coats following them must have been prodigious. But under the vigorous rule first of Henry Phillpotts and then of Frederick Temple most of them disappeared from the hunting field. There is the famous story of how Phillpotts asked Russell to give up his pack of hounds as a personal favour to himself. Russell agreed and the two men shook hands. Then the parson said: 'I won't deceive you—not for the world, my lord. I'll give up the pack sure enough —but Mrs Russell will keep it instead of me.'

In the heyday of the hunting parson it was not uncommon for notices like the following one at Redbourn in Hertfordshire, to be given out by the Parish Clerk in church: 'The Vicar is goin' on Friday to the throwin'-off of the Leicestershire 'ounds; consequently he will not be back till Monday next week. Therefore next Sunday there will be no sarvice in this church on that day.' The medieval 'Parson Hogg', as recorded in Baring-Gould's *Songs of the West*, when he heard the hunting horn was not prepared to wait even to complete a wedding service:

> He shut his book. 'Come on', he said,
> 'I'll pray and bless no more sir!'
> He drew the surplice o'er his head,
> And started for the door, sir.

His nineteenth-century successor was more accommodating, remaining until after the ceremony was completed:

> Says he, for your welfare I'll pray;
> I regret I no longer can stay.
> Now youre safely made one,
> I must quickly be gone;
> For I must go a hunting today.

But perhaps the keenest clerical huntsman of all time was the blind Edward Stokes, the eighteenth-century Rector of Blaby in Leicestershire, who rode to hounds with a groom at his side, and jumped the hedges when the latter gave the signal by ringing a bell. Hunting, indeed, could become an obsession and a full-time occupation; and more than justified Bishop Phillpotts's celebrated remark to a clergyman of Froude's kidney: 'I don't complain of your hunting, but that you do nothing else.' Another bishop is reported to have said to one of his sporting parsons: 'If you can assure me that you can spare the time and the money, that you can take a day's holiday in the week without neglecting your duties, reducing your charities, or getting into debt, you have my permission to hunt on one immutable condition: that you ride straight to hounds and if I hear of you craving or shirking, I shall withdraw it at once.'

Hunting parsons probably lingered on longest in East Anglia and the Home Counties, particularly perhaps in Essex, where I personally well remember the Reverend A. Oliver of Latton, who died in 1942 at the ripe old age of eighty. His tiny parish required little supervision; and regularly every winter he turned out to hunt with the Essex fox hounds, while spending his summer afternoons on the tennis court. The only time I ever heard him take a service he had finished and departed from the church before many of the congregation had realized he had properly begun. 'Only a very bold or a very foolish parishioner', wrote William Addison, 'would have asked him to take a wedding or a funeral on a day when he had a hunt in prospect.' From Essex, too, comes the oft told tale of how the Reverend Sir Henry Bute Dudley of Bradwell-on-sea finished a run by killing the fox on the chancel roof of Cricksea church. Few clergymen, one imagines, hunt today. The expense would be too great for one thing; and anyway most modern parsons are drawn from a different social class and have been trained in a very different school of thought from their eighteenth- and nineteenth-century predecessors.

Shooting, fishing, and coursing were certainly regarded as more respectable pursuits for the clergy than hunting; particularly when they were working their own glebe and were more concerned with securing cheap food for the pot than with the sport itself. Parson Woodeforde, it may be remembered, was extremely fond of coursing a hare. But the country-gentleman-cleric of the nineteenth century was frequently called upon to carry a gun at big country house shooting parties, where the question of food was a purely secondary one. The slaughter, indeed, was tremendous. Archdeacon Philpot of Great Cressingham in Norfolk recorded in his journal an account of one such shoot undertaken by the Barings in the 'fifties, when 610 brace of partridges were killed by five sportsmen in a single day. He also noted his friend Sir Francis Goodriche's game book for the four years: 1847-51. 'Pheasants 6,581, partridges 5,713, hares 5,705, rabbits 13,825.' The Reverend Giles Daubeney, Vicar of Herne from 1905 to 1945, was a fine shot. He always sent Archbishop Lang some pheasants and woodcock for Christmas; and an occasional salmon to his old friend, the Vicar of Yalding. The latter presented one of these fish to his Bishop, and within a fortnight was made a Canon! So common, in fact, became the sight of a clerical collar at a shoot, that its absence was sometimes a source of relief. Giles Daubeney once told the following story: 'During a big country house shoot', he said, 'we were all standing round the dinningroom table waiting for the squire to give the signal to commence luncheon. This he did, after glancing round and ejaculating, "Thank God no damned parsons". I was, of course, not wearing clerical dress at the time.'

Perhaps the country clergy of Victorian England were particularly addicted to the so-called gentle art of fishing; although actually this is one of the cruellest sports in the world. Sydney Smith wrote in the *Edinburgh Review:* 'Running an iron hook in the intestines of an animal; presenting this first animal to another as his food; and then pulling this second creature up and suspending him by the barb in his stomach . . . these cruelties pass under the pretty name of angling.' Nevertheless it became a favourite clerical pastime, whether like Robert Martin of Challacombe you expertly fished the trout streams of Exmoor; or caught pike like Robert Hart of Takeley in the depths of Hatfield Forest lake; or travelled north with Richard Seymour of Kinwarton as far as Scotland in order to do battle with the salmon. Others, like Horace Rackham of High Wych, contented themselves with spending a pleasant summer's afternoon sitting on the banks of a neighbouring pool or river, with a book in one hand and a fishing rod in the other!

The clerical fisherman has, of course, a long tradition behind him. The medieval priest indulged in the sport for reasons of both profit and pleasure. It was said, for example, of the curate of Loughborough in 1518: 'he . . . abandons himself to games and jesting, nor will he leave them to visit a sick parishioner. . . . He gives himself to fishing and fowling, and, if he knows that there is a sick person to be visited or a little child to be christened, then will he be off to his fishing and fowling and tell the other chaplains to minister these sacraments, and that habitually'; while Sir George, curate of Barton-on-Humber about the same date, was described as, 'a common fisherman and went out wading'.

The country parson, one has to admit, is a gambler at heart despite all the episcopal tirades against games of chance. Even today, in the face of a good deal of official displeasure, raffles and draws continue to flourish at Christmas bazaars and garden fetes; and these events would not be the financial successes that they are without them. Such a reliance on 'Providence' is possibly derived from the old farming days when so much had to be wagered on the vagaries of the English climate. Medieval clerks had to be reprimanded for playing chess for money on Sunday mornings, or throwing dice. When cards appeared they quickly became popular. The Rector of Normanton at the beginning of the seventeenth century was caught 'playing at the tables with the Scholemaster of Hambleton', instead of taking his Sunday services. And this kind of thing was made a common complaint by the Puritans against the country clergy some forty years later, who were severely dealt with by the parliamentary sequestration committees. In the eighteenth century clerical gamblers were all too common. One has only to recall that hardened sinner Parson Sampson out of *The Virginians;* the innumerable hours spent by Parson Woodeforde at the card table; and George Crabbe's 'jovial youth', who 'skilled at whist, devotes the night to play'. The 'reformed' Victorian parson might eschew gambling; but he still took pleasure in the family rubber of whist. And all too many modern clergymen turn out to patronize the village whist-drive.

As the nineteenth century wore on a growing number of public-school incumbents came into their livings full of a 'games' enthusiasm; and proceeded to teach their parishioners how to play cricket and football. Unorganized football had been played for centuries in the countryside and many parsons had participated. Sir Richard, curate of Hawridge in 1518, was presented for playing football in his shirt; while we have already heard of how the Vicar of Charlton in Oxfordshire, early in the seventeenth century, with another man, 'did play togeather against William Witham and Thomas Preist . . . att football' when, alas, he was somewhat the worse for liquor. Now, however, such play became 'organized' and much more genteel. The Hon. Edward Bligh, Vicar of Birling in Kent from 1865 to 1875, was a first class bat, who played a lot of public cricket, and ended his career in this field during Canterbury Week, 1862, when he helped to represent an England XI against 'fourteen of Kent', made fifty-two runs, and was eventually bowled by a very slow lob. He started up cricket clubs in both his country livings of Rotherfield in Sussex and Birling in Kent where he also played himself. Less gifted players often felt constrained to do likewise. The Revd James Lee Warner recounted in his *Parochalia* how in a match between his own Dorsetshire village of Tarrant Gunville and its neighbour of Chettle in the 'eighties, the Vicar of Chettle made 103 runs and took eight Gunville wickets. Charles Kingsley even permitted Sunday evening cricket. 'Eh, Parson', remarked the village publican, ' 'ee don't objec', not he, as loik as not 'e'll come and look on, and 'ee do tell 'em as it's a deal better to 'ave a bit of 'ealthy play o' a Sunday evening than to be a-larking 'ere and a-larking there all over the place a-courting and a-drinking ale.'

Today the names of cricketing parsons are legion, ranging from the genius of David Sheppard to that humbler brother, of whom William Addison wrote: 'I watched such a village parson, a lanky old bachelor of seventy, with tousled grey hair, and old-fashioned spectacles slipping down his nose, hitting boundaries on a village green to the delight of cheering schoolboys.' Perhaps, sometimes, he takes the game too seriously. 'The Christian Life! What is it?' the Revd Septimus Jones used to ask from the pulpit; and then with a beaming smile answered his own question. It was the 'Great Game': 'A struggle against odds on a bad wicket, sometimes in a poor light, against venomous bowling if the Devil was in the field, and against powerful and merciless batting if he was at the wicket.'

Archery came into vogue. Canon Seymour speaks of many a tournament attended by his family at the stately homes of Worcestershire and Warwickshire; while at Clyro the Revd Francis Kilvert took particular pleasure in acting as the ladies' 'quiver', holding their arrows for them as they shot at the mark. But late in the nineteenth century croquet became adopted as the clerical pastime par excellence. 'There is something infinitely attractive', wrote Canon P. B. G. Binnall, 'in the picture of sedate tea and croquet parties on the spacious lawns of many a Lincolnshire Rectory, which contemporary diaries and letters give us.' That undoubtedly was the feeling at the time. Perhaps, however, an older school of thought, reared in the hunting, shooting, and fishing traditions of an earlier age, might find something ludicrous in the sight of 'a short, stout man wandering among the croquet hoops in a cassock'.

Whatever the New Canons may have to say about the clergy donning lay attire for the purpose of 'innocent recreation'; the very fact that they do so endears them to their parishioners and helps to consolidate their influence in their villages. A countryman certainly does not want his priest to be always on duty, clothed in cassock and surplice, saying his prayers and taking his services. A country parson who does not smoke, drink, play games, or gossip is not usually a very popular figure, however good a preacher or ardent a ritualist he may be. Every parishioner needs his priest as a priest at one time or another, in church or in the privacy of his own house; but he will then like him all the better and find his ministrations the more effective, if their previous acquaintanceship had been formed in the realm of the human and the fallible, whose frailties, while they do not in the least dim the aura of the *persona*, yet help to bridge the gulf between the mortal and the divine. It was not for nothing that Dean Hole related the story of the clerical batsman, who converted a villager by the preliminary method of knocking him out by a vicious hook to leg. This man, who was a miner and violently anti-clerical, suddenly saw the light; but on being asked by the parson what had caused his amazing change of heart, he replied: 'Oh, that hit o' yourn to square leg for six converted me.'

# CHAPTER VI

# Odd Man Out

THE COUNTRY CLERGY have long been famous for fostering a spirit of eccentricity and producing a remarkable line of 'characters'. Eccentricity may, of course, entail anything from a conscious desire to 'show off' or to be 'out of the ordinary', to frustrated genius or a touch of real madness. It is, in fact, a very wide term embracing a multitude of sins and virtues. For genius, it has been said, is closely akin to madness; and a man, who perhaps has been born a century too soon and finds himself compelled to stand idly by while a life's work is thwarted of its fruits and a splendid vision turned into a mirage in face of an obstinate conservatism, might well be driven over the thin line that divides the sane from the insane, and separates the normal from the abnormal.

No doubt many noted parson 'characters' would have proved themselves to be out of the ordinary in any other walk of life; yet the twin but contrasting circumstances of the often extreme isolation of their pastoral charges and their own supreme importance within their narrow boundaries, facilitated the growth of oddities and eccentrics. The country incumbent was perhaps the only educated man in his village, its spiritual and often its secular leader. Anything he did or did not do would probably go unquestioned. He could indulge his whims, try out his experiments, exploit his ego to the full without fear of rebuke or criticism, provided he did not seriously offend against tradition or the laws of Church and State. All that was true of the past, particularly of the eighteenth and nineteenth centuries; but it is certainly not true today, when villages are no longer isolated; villagers are no longer uneducated, credulous, and subservient; and above all the parson himself is no longer the independent power in the Community that he once was. He is now overshadowed by both the diocese and the welfare state. He must mind his ps and qs, keep in step, and pursue a conventional course; or woe betide him.

In medieval times the country priest, ignorant as he might appear to his ecclesiastical superiors, was usually the only man of cultivated intelligence within his tiny parish of three or four hundred souls, which was cut off from the next village by many miles of forest, swamp, or moor. Born a peasant, with all a peasant's ingrained knowledge of country lore and superstition, it was unlikely that the little learning he had picked up on his way to the priesthood would make any fundamental change in his character and outlook. Nevertheless he could no longer meet his neighbours on quite the old footing or accept life quite as they accepted it. He was forced back upon himself; and, if a man of somewhat unusual intelligence, he might well begin questioning and probing into Life's secrets, trying to fit his book-learning and the teaching of the Church into his own intuitive knowledge of Nature and of the pagan superstitions that had been handed down from immemorial times, and were in the blood of every serf. As a priest he was expected to use the 'white' magic of the Church to enforce discipline and quell disobedience; and there were wonderful stories abroad of its effectiveness. Excommunication was certainly a terrible weapon.

> Thou shalt pronounce this hideous thing,
> With cross and candle and bell-knelling.
> Speak out clearly, fear not thou wound,
> That all may thee understand.

The excommunicated person was cursed 'within and without, sleeping or waking, going and sitting, standing and riding, lying above earth and under earth, speaking and crying and drinking; in wood, in water, in field, in town.' Furthermore he could take no part in 'mass or mattins nor of none other good prayers that be done in holy Church nor in none other places, but that the pains of hell be their meed with Judas that betrayed our Lord Jesus Christ.'

> Then thou thy candle shalt thou cast to ground,
> And spit thereto the same stound [hour]
> And let also the belles knell
> To make their heartes the more grill [afraid].

Such a curse could have terrible consequences. When on Christmas night 1013 a mob of riotous carollers invaded their parish church, linking hands and dancing up and down, instead of hearing Mass, the parish priest excommunicated them. Immediately their hands became inseparably joined and remained so for a whole year. The knowledge that he possessed, or thought he possessed, these powers might lead the parson into strange paths himself. In 1530 a priest, Thomas Pett, was charged at Lincoln before the Vicar-General with using charms and incantations to recover lost property; and in some places the clergy were reported to be able to cast the evil eye, so that 'when men meet priests the first thing in the morning they cross themselves, saying it is an evil omen to meet a priest'. In one village, which had been stricken by the plague, it was believed that the deadly visitation would not cease until the parson had been buried alive. 'Whence it came to pass that, when the priest came to the edge of the grave to bury a dead parishioner, then the country folk, men and women together, seized him, arrayed as he was in his priestly vestments, and cast him into the pit.'

John Buchan in *Witch Wood*, writing of a later age, reminds us how easily in an isolated, beforested community such things could and did happen. Here, indeed, the pastor was on the side of the angels. But Nathaniel Hawthorne, describing a similar scene in New England, found the clergy themselves the organizers of Satanism: 'At one extremity of an open space, hemmed in by the dark wall of forest, rose a rock, bearing some rude, natural resemblance either to an altar or a pulpit and surrounded by four blazing pines . . . as the red light rose and fell appeared the faces which Sabbath after Sabbath looked devoutly heavenward, and benignantly over the crowded pews, from the holiest pulpits in the land.' A modern novelist tells the story of an extreme Anglo-Catholic incumbent, who first emptied his country church by his pseudo-Romanist practices, and then filled it again by resorting to the black arts of the Middle Ages. No doubt such tales were based on at least a modicum of fact; and reveal practices that were not unknown in medieval, seventeenth century, and even more modern times, although they were rarely uncovered or publicized.

None the less, occasionally faint whispers of the performance of pagan rites, or other queer stories concerning certain parsons, would leak out in visitation returns. The notorious Dr John Dee, Rector of Leadenham, for example, was thus described in the Lincoln *Liber Cleri* of 1576: 'Does not reside; neither is he in holy orders; vehemently suspected in religion; an astronomer, not a theologian'. Dee is an interesting character, whose genuine interest in astrology and spiritualism was twisted by his enemies into traffic with the black arts. Although the nominal Rector of Upton-on-Severn as well as Leadenham, the astrologer was never ordained, for as he said to Queen Elizabeth: 'A cura animarum annexa did terrifie me to deal with them'. He settled instead at Mortlake, where he collected a famous library, cast horoscopes, practised astrology, and dabbled in spiritualism. He himself was no medium; but employed a succession of 'skryers', particularly a certain Kelley, through whose powers he sought to find the means to manufacture gold. At Mortlake he was visited by the Queen, became her astrologer, and supplied her with valuable information. For instance he claimed to have seen the forthcoming execution of Mary Queen of Scots and the defeat of the Armada. Dee was in touch with all the leading Elizabethans, most of whom were his friends; and he acquired a considerable reputation abroad, travelling widely through Europe. Eventually he received the Wardenship of Manchester College as a reward for his arduous labours. He died in 1608. Perhaps the most colourful episode in his life was his acceptance of the 'spirits' command, translated through the rascally medium Kelley, to indulge with the latter in a literal communism, wherein they shared not only their possessions, but their wives! There is little doubt that Dee was a genuine and learned seeker after truth; but in the popular mind he was a wizard. On one occasion his house at Mortlake was sacked by the mob; while he himself was more than once accused by his enemies of witchcraft. However, he was invariably and fully cleared of any such taint. How far it is fair to claim Dee as a country parson is open to question; but he certainly held country benefices, and lived on their incomes.

During the Civil Wars John Lowes, Vicar of Brandeston in Suffolk, was arraigned for witchcraft and executed at Bury St Edmunds in August 1645. He confessed to having bewitched a ship near Harwich that went down with all hands; and further admitted, 'he had done many other hanous, wicked and accursed acts by the help of Six Impes which he had that frequented him daily'. It was, in fact, actually alleged that he had made a covenant with the Devil and was marked by Satan with teats on the crown of his head and under his tongue. Joseph Harrison, Vicar of Sustead in Norfolk, had earlier appeared before the Court of High Commission charged with being 'a professor of the Art Magick and in particular, charmeing of piggs'.

The tradition of the country priest who was in league with the Devil and could cast the evil eye, has persisted into modern times. R. D. Blackmore drew such a character, which was taken from real life, in the person of Parson Chowne, who played a prominent part in his *Maid of Sker*. John Mitford, the poet, writer, collector, and landscape gardener, who was Vicar of Benhall and Rector of Stratford St Andrew in Suffolk for forty-nine years during the first half of the nineteenth century, enjoyed a similar reputation. He is still referred to locally as 'the wicked old parson, who haunts Mitford Lane.' A contemporary Rector of Dunkerton in Cornwall, the Reverend C. F. Bampfylde, was commonly known as 'the Devil of Dunkerton'; and was once described by a fellow cleric as the worst man in the West of England.

It is hardly likely that there are any country clergy of the kidney of Parsons Bampfylde or Froude about today; but Satanism itself is certainly not dead. According to the late Reverend Montague Summers it is still extensively practised in England. He wrote in his book, *Witchcraft and Black Magic*: 'They may call it psychism or occultism; they may learn to cast curses or spells; they may invoke the help of the powers of evil, but it is practically the same thing, and its lure to mankind is as old and mysterious as the wind that blows over the earth, urging them with strange elusive thrills to recapture and use the old powers of the Serpent.'

From magic it is no far cry to madness, which has not infrequently cropped up in country parsonages, where a naturally unstable mind has been further weakened by isolation, domestic tragedy, or some parochial crisis. At Bingham in Nottinghamshire in the year 1743 the Rector was Henry Stanhope, the natural son of the second Earl of Chesterfield. Stanhope had expected a substantial legacy from his father; and when he found himself cut right out of the will, he went out of his mind. 'The Rector', his curate informed the Archbishop of York, 'has been for many years with an uncommon Phrensy. He resides in his Parsonage House.' According to a very strong tradition Stanhope used to ride round his parish clad in white breeches and astride a large white mule as a sign of mourning for his loss. There are plenty of more modern examples. A lunatic rector inhabited a little village near Gainsborough during the 'eighties; and about the same date a deranged Vicar of Laxton in Northamptonshire burnt the ancient church registers because, he declared, they contained much that was evil. When Edward King became Bishop of Lincoln he was informed that his clergy could be divided into three categories: those who had gone out of their minds; those who were about to go out of their minds; and those who had no minds to go out of. Finally, one can recall a country rector of more recent date, who periodically imagined that he was a millionaire, when he would place orders for such items as yachts and race-horses. As a rule these 'mad' parsons were harmless enough; although at times they could be a source of embarrassment to the diocesan authorities or their own parishioners. I have never heard of a homicidal maniac installed in a parsonage.

The sadist, however, was a different proposition altogether. He, alas, has certainly not been unknown in the country parsonage, including the wife-beater, the flogging schoolmaster, the bullying employer, and the tyrannical parent, who delighted in inflicting pain and suffering, both physical and mental. Yet, strange as it may seem, he was usually able to convince himself, and so salve his conscience, that what he was doing was for the ultimate benefit of his victim. Jeremiah Ravens, Rector of Great Blakenham in Suffolk, was deprived of his living in 1644 because he 'hunge his wife upp by the heels and tyed her to the bedposts and whipped her'. But perhaps the most glaring example of this kind of unpleasant eccen-

tricity was to be found in the person of Canon Thomas Butler of
Langar in Nottinghamshire, whom his son, Samuel Butler, por-
trayed in *The Way of All Flesh*. 'Before Ernest could well crawl he
was taught to kneel; before he could well speak he was taught to
lisp the Lord's Prayer, and the General Confession. How was it
possible that these things could be taught too early? If his attention
flagged or his memory failed him here was an ill weed which
would grow apace, unless it were plucked out immediately, and the
only way to pluck it out was to whip him, or shut him up in a cup-
board, or dock him of some of the small pleasures of childhood.
Before he was three years old he could read and, after a fashion,
write. Before he was four he was learning Latin and could do rule
of three sums. . . . He was fond of his mother, but as regards his
father, he has told me in later life he could remember no feeling but
fear and shrinking. Christina did not remonstrate with Theobald
concerning the severity of the tasks imposed upon their boy, nor
yet as to the continual whippings that were found necessary at lesson
times. Indeed, when during any absence of Theobald's the lessons
were entrusted to her, she found to her sorrow that it was the only
thing to do, and she did it no less effectively than Theobald himself;
nevertheless she was fond of her boy, which Theobald never was,
and it was long before she could destroy all affection for herself in the
mind of her first-born. But she persevered.' None the less the Reverend Theobald Pontifex of Battersby-on-the-hill was a just and con-
siderate employer; and he was not actively disliked by his parishioners.
But the sadistic streak was there and he vented it on his family.

The humorous and lovable Sydney Smith had a similar kink in
his nature. On one occasion he compelled a little girl, whom he had
caught biting into a peach in his garden, to stand for a whole day in
the middle of his lawn, with a placard round her neck containing the
single word 'Thief'. Alexander Lendrum, Rector of Blatherwycke
towards the end of the nineteenth century, is chiefly remembered in
the village today for a spiteful daughter, whose hard, scientific
pinches stimulated the brains of dull Sunday School scholars. In
conclusion one might cite the particularly atrocious behaviour of
Parson Froude of Knowstone. Froude, who disliked his curate,
made him drunk one Sunday between services, and then caused him
to be hung up in an empty corn-sack from a beam in an out-house.
While this was still going on the bells began ringing for Evensong;
but when the congregation assembled there was no-one to officiate.
The curate could not, and Froude would not, conduct the service.
Froude delighted in inflicting pain. Blackmore tells the story of how
he sold a horse to a Devonshire baronet, but placed hemp-seeds
under the lids of its eyes. The seeds burst and drove the horse mad;

the baronet was thrown and badly injured; and the horse itself had
to be shot.

What exactly produces the clerical sartorial rebel? Is it vanity, a
desire to show off, or a need for greater comfort? Perhaps he feels
that by dressing as a layman he thereby becomes a better mixer or
more effectively asserts the sturdy independence of his character.
Whatever the cause he has a long tradition behind him. During the
Middle Ages a dire struggle went on between the Church Authorities on the one side and the parochial clergy on the other over the
latter's costume or lack of it. Undoubtedly at one time there was a
widespread refusal to wear the clerical habit or submit to the tonsure.
An injunction of John Stratford, Archbishop of Canterbury, in
1342 declared: 'Parsons holding ecclesiastical dignities, rectories
. . . benefices with cure of souls; even men in Holy Orders, scorn to
wear the tonsure, which is the crown of the Kingdom of Heaven
and of perfection, and distinguish themselves by hair spreading to
the shoulders in an effeminate manner, and walk about clad in a
military rather than a clerical dress, with an outer habit very short
and tight-fitting, but excessively wide, with long sleeves which do
not touch the elbow; their hair curled and perfumed, their hoods
with lappets of wonderful length; with long beards, rings on their
fingers, and girded belts with precious stones of wonderful size,
their purses enamelled and gilt with various devices and knives
openly hanging at them like swords, their boots red and green
peaked and cut in many ways; with housings to their saddles, and
horns hanging from their necks; their capes and cloaks so furred, in
rash disregard of the Canons, that there appears little or no distinc-
tion between clergyman and layman.' Yet all attempts to get the
sumptuary Canons strictly enforced failed. One bishop, after
reading these Canons at a visitation, ordered that the hair of his
clergy was to be cut then and there on the spot. Bishop Grostete of
Lincoln once refused to institute a cleric who arrived untonsured,
clad in scarlet, and wearing rings. In fact there were all too many
medieval priests who sought to ape their lay social superiors in
manners, dress, and deportment; while reluctantly conceding as
little as possible to the laws of the Church. For instance they would
wear a special headcovering, known as the 'priests' bonnet', in
order to conceal the tonsure, a coloured instead of a grey or black
habit, and a short sword or knife hanging from the girdle in place
of the normal string of beads. William Langland wrote of them:

> Sloth with his sling a hard assault he made,
> Proud priests came with him more than a thousand,
> In cloaks and peaked shoes and pissers' long knives.

Such worldly and unlearned clerics, he added, would never do any good in the world:

> Unless many a priest bore instead of their daggers and their
>     brooches,
> A set of beads in their hand and a book under their arm.
> Sir John and Sir Geoffrey have a girdle of silver,
> A dagger or a knife with studs guilded.
> But a breviary that should be his plow. . . .

In Queen Elizabeth's reign William Harrison, the knowledgeable Rector of Radwinter, compared the 'comely apparell' of his Puritan friends with the gorgeous appearance of the medieval priest. 'To meet a priest in those days', he declared, 'was to behold a peacocke that spreadeth his taile when he danseth before the henne.' Harrison's friends, however, could scarcely have included John Birkbie, Rector of Moor-Monkton in Yorkshire, who in 1567 was reported to be using 'very undecent apparell namelie great britches cut and drawne oute with sarcenet and taffite and great ruffes laid on with laceis of gold and silk'. The Royal Injunctions of 1559 had laid down that the clergy were to wear the cassock, gown, tippet, and square cap; and the diocese of Lincoln at any rate insisted upon a subscription to the following declaration before a cleric could be admitted to any office: 'I shall use sobrietie in apparell and speciallie in the Church at common praiers according to order appointed.' Canon 74 of the Canons of 1604 decreed that ministers should wear, *inter alia*, square caps and, when on a journey, 'cloaks with sleeves, commonly called priests' cloaks, without guards, welts, long buttons, or cuts.' At home their clothes might not be 'cut or pinkt', and they were forbidden to wear any light-coloured stockings, coifs, or wrought night-caps. Only plain night-caps were permitted of 'black silk, satin, or velvet'. William Wood, Rector of Somerby in Leicestershire, was actually presented by his churchwardens in 1607 for 'wearinge a wrought night-cap'. The Canons, in fact, were by no means strictly observed; and when the Reverend Dr William Slater appeared before the Star Chamber in 1631 to answer various charges made against him, Laud, then Bishop of London, reproved him severely for dressing like a layman. 'Ministers', said the Bishop, 'should be more careful in their habits and not to goe like rufflers as if they were ashamed of their ministry.' Dr Slater excused himself on the grounds that these were his riding clothes, and that he had only just alighted from his horse. Such a flimsy argument did not impress Laud, who promptly retorted, 'that if he sawe him in the like hereafter he would looke out some canon or other to take hould of him'.

During the Civil Wars lay attire sometimes helped the parson to escape the attentions of his Roundhead enemies. When, for instance, in 1656 soldiers came to arrest Guy Carleton, Vicar of Bucklebury in Berkshire, they mistook him for a servant since 'he wore a grey coat and had his boots on'. And so he escaped, at least for the moment.

After the Restoration, particularly in the latter half of the eighteenth century, a not inconsiderable number of worldly parsons dressed and acted like laymen of the worst type. In a sermon, later printed under the general title: *Clerical Misconduct Reprobated*, which was preached at an archidecanal visitation in June, 1787, such worldly clerics were attacked in no uncertain terms. 'One day in the week', declared the preacher, 'they are clergymen, and all the rest of it mere lay men, men of the world. Indeed the clergyman is a character they are most ashamed of, and which, there is reason to think, some would actually disclaim, were it consistent with their interest.'

The Evangelical Revival and the Oxford Movement, by encouraging a more serious approach to religion, both personal and corporate, created a fashion for greater uniformity and sobriety in clerical dress. The Victorian country clergy on the whole were impeccably and conventionally attired. None the less the unconventional parson, the rebel, and the freak have always been with us. R. S. Hawker of Morwenstow was conspicuously unconventional in the matter of his dress. At first he wore a simple brown cassock, 'the hue of Our Lady's hair'; but later on he changed it for a long coat of purple shade, a fisherman's blue jersey with a small red cross on the side where the Centurion had pierced Jesus with his spear, a limp white cravat, Hessian boots, and a wide-awake hat. From his button-hole hung a broad carpenter's pencil to remind him of the Carpenter's Shop; and when he went walking he carried a cross-handled stick. Some of the neighbouring clergy commented a little unkindly on this unusual attire; whereupon Hawker retorted: 'I don't make myself look like a waiter-out-of-place or an unemployed undertaker, and that I do scrupulously abide by the injunctions of the 74th Canon of 1604.'

The new Canons at present before the Convocations contain one, No. 84, that deals with the minister's dress. This carefully explains in its preamble that the main objective is, 'to have them known to the people, and thereby to receive the honour and estimation due to the special messengers and ministers of Almighty God'. It further demands that every clergyman should 'wear such apparel as shall be suitable to the gravity of his office.' Maybe there is a need for such a Canon. In reaction no doubt against Victorian and Edwardian uniformity and conventionality, the country clergy today often display the strangest appearance. Some rarely don the clerical collar; and, indeed, the exhibition ranges widely from parsons of the type of the late Conrad Noel, who walk abroad clothed in the full habit of the medieval priest, to the hatless, collarless, corduroy-trousered, fancy-shirted rector of broad views in more senses than one.

The physician-parson can perhaps hardly be termed an oddity, since he has a long and honourable record behind him; although, of course, he is seldom found in this country today. In this highly specialized age he is no longer required except possibly in the realm of psychiatry and faith-healing. But in the unspecialized, less complicated, less knowledgeable and far more credulous past he played an important and useful rôle in the village, where he could and did bury his own mistakes. George Herbert wrote of his ideal priest: 'The Country Parson desires to be all to his parish, and not only a pastor, but a lawyer also, and a physician. . . . If there be any of his flock sick, he is their physician, or at least his wife, of whom instead of the qualities of the world, he asks no other, but to have the skill of healing a wound, or helping the sick. But if neither himself, nor his wife have the skill, and his means serve, he keeps some young practitioner in his house for the benefit of his parish. . . . Yet it is easy for any scholar to attain to such a measure of physic, as may be of much use to him both for himself, and others. This is done by seeing one anatomy, reading one book of physic, having one herbal by him.'

Eighteenth-century clerical diaries reveal that these words had been taken to heart. James Woodeforde in his rôle of Good Samaritan doctored his parishioners with herbs and simples. Benjamin Rogers was more ambitious. 'Ordered William Allen of Bridgend to be blooded for the Pleurisie', he recorded in his journal for 1 April 1729. During the next two days he ordered him to be blooded again; and on the fourth day the wretched William Allen died. In all some thirty ounces of blood were drawn. The recipes Rogers prescribed for quite common ailments or accidents were often formidable in the extreme. The bite of a mad dog, for example, he suggested ought to be treated in the following manner: 'Take (having washed the blood from the wound) of ash-coloured Liverwort reduced to powder, two drams, of black pepper beaten to powder 4 drams. Mix and divide this into 6 parts and take one every morning in a pint of warm milk.' George Crabbe, who was a doctor by profession, having earned his living in that capacity for many years before his ordination, was strangely enough neither as popular nor as successful as some of the amateurs. At Aldesburgh in Suffolk, where he first practised, he was described as being, 'but poorly qualified for his profession, his skill in surgery being notably deficient. He attracted only the poorest class of patients'. So, at a later date, his parishioners at Muston were probably no better off than those of Rogers at Carlton. Another bold practitioner was Benjamin Philpot at Great Cressinham cum Bodney. 'On one occasion', he wrote in his diary, 'a woman, who had a son subject to the falling sickness [epilepsy], came and asked for "half-a-crown taken at the Holy Table", bringing the equivalent in small change. She wanted it to make a ring out of it for her son's small finger. I told her I could give her something better than that, though I let her try this at least harmless charm, but when satisfied of its failure she returned it to me, I tried my usual remedy with the usual measure of relief. I always kept a number of simple remedies, chiefly the tincture of herbs, but I was sometimes puzzled at the names they gave their complaints. Will Green came to me one day, full of pain with his hand on his stomach. "Please, Sir, I've got the flickers." Being at a loss I tried four grains of rhubarb, which at any rate proved an effective solution. Brandy and salt was much given in those days and I used it a good deal. On one occasion I was going out and had no time to mix them, but gave John Coggles the brandy and said, "Here, John, you can mix the salt with this yourself". Next day I met him and hoped he had mixed the ingredients properly. 'Well, Sir, they got mixed. I drank the brandy first and eat the salt with my victuals; I was sure they'd come together".'

Church authorities did not always approve of this invasion by the clergy of other men's occupations. They were expected to stick to their own calling and not 'to use themselves as laymen'. In 1597, after Bishop Redman's visitation of the Norwich diocese, Robert Wattkinson, curate of Dunwich, was presented and admonished because, or so it was alleged, he 'practizeth physicke'. However, such a knowledge of medicine enabled a number of incumbents, who were evicted under the Commonwealth and Protectorate, to earn their living and thus keep their heads above the financial waters until the King enjoyed his own again.

Sydney Smith, Rector of Foston-le-Clay in Yorkshire and later of Combe Florey near Taunton in the early nineteenth century, particularly prided himself on his success as a physician. At Foston he used his study for housing all kinds of queer medical apparatus, as for instance a suit not unlike a diver's, which was filled with hot water and called 'his rheumatic armour'. He built himself an apothecary's shop while at Combe Florey, where any of his parishioners could be sure of obtaining free medicines. Called one day to baptise a dying infant, Smith recorded in his journal: 'I first gave it a dose of castor-oil, and then I christened it; so now the poor child is ready for either world.' He invented a stomach pump, which he tried out, quite successfully, on one of his footmen who had swallowed some arsenic by accident. Sydney Smith was a true eccentric. He farmed his own glebe in Yorkshire; and used to direct his labourers from a huge speaking trumpet sited outside his front door. He also watched them through a telescope from his study window to see if they were doing their work properly. One harvest, in an emergency, he saved his crops 'by injecting large quantities of fermented liquor into the workmen and making them work all night'. And in order to prevent his cattle rubbing themselves against the trees, he installed in the fields what he called a 'universal scratcher'. Indeed, stories about Sydney Smith's activities as a country parson are endless; and the same could be said of any other well-known parsonic 'character'.

The task of unravelling the full quota of parsonic eccentricity would take a life-time of study and fill several volumes. Here it must be sufficient to add that, with some obvious exceptions, such eccentricities have probably done more good than harm in the countryside as a whole. The fact that Hawker kept nine or ten cats which followed him to church and careered about in it during service time; that Francis Pickford, the aged Rector of Hagworth-ingham, tamed squirrels during the eighteen-eighties; that Edmond Long of White Roothing was fond of kissing little girls; and that Samuel Parr used to smoke his pipe in the vestry and sometimes during intervals in the service itself, would as like as not be the kind of traits to endear rather than repel. Certainly no-one at the beginning of the nineteenth century thought the Romney Marsh parson odd, who, on the way to the pulpit, would lean over his churchwarden's pew and make some such observation as: 'Well, Smithers, I'll have that pig'. Many characters of this type were no doubt deliberately cultivated, and were the hall-mark of a sturdy, rustic independence. These were men who could never have been described in any servile sense as the delegates of the Bishop. They said what they thought, and acted on their own initiative by the light of their own consciences.

CHAPTER VII

# The Economic Background

THE PRINCIPAL SOURCES of the country parson's income have varied very little from Anglo-Saxon to quite modern times. They consisted of glebe, the land with which the parish church was originally endowed by its patron; of tithe, which at least from the Lateran Council of 1180 was compulsorily paid to the incumbent; and of an assortment of fees, offerings, and oblations due to him from his flock on certain occasions and at fixed festivals. After the Reformation there were also some augmentations. These last were voluntarily contributed by the patron and parishioners, or originated in state schemes like the grants made by the Long Parliament out of confiscated royalist impropriations, or the more permanent gifts from the famous Queen Anne's Bounty, which was established in 1704.

The medieval priest lived, as has already been seen, a very simple life; and his economic standards were not dissimilar from those of his people. His house was small and rude, and contained little more than the necessities of life; his clothing was rough but durable and could be worn for years on end; and his day, apart from his religious duties, was spent labouring in the fields. He rose at day-break and retired to bed early, thus saving both light and fuel; his food was homely, the product of his own efforts or those of his neighbours; and his recreations would consist of little more than joining in the village sports and pastimes or drinking at the alehouse. Consequently he had little need for money, except to pay his taxes or purchase luxuries. But such simple living, alas, did not engender in the country clergy as a whole a spirit of Christian charity and generosity. The picture that has come down to us is of the parson enforcing every tittle of his rights under pain of excommunication by bell, book, and candle; and of the Church as a whole insisting upon tithe being paid even unto the uttermost farthing. This policy of grab and greed built up against the clergy, at first slowly and inarticulately but none the less formidably, a mountain of ill-will. William Langland wrote in the fourteenth century:

If priests were perfect they would no silver take
For masses nor for matins and not their meat of usurers,

Nor neither their kirtle nor coat though they for cold should
die,
If they their duty did. . . .

Such anti-clericalism grew alarmingly after the Reformation,
when the barriers were at last down, and led eventually in our own
times to the abandonment of tithe-collecting altogether in exchange
for a totally inadequate compensation. The clergy claimed that by
divine law, based on scriptural precedent, the crops grown by the
husbandman, the young of his flocks and herds, pigs and poultry,
and even the profits of craftsmen and tradesmen were subject to the
Church's tax of ten per cent. But they went further than this.
Orchards were raided and the little gardens where a man grew a
few vegetables. If he felled a tree that was not of twenty years
growth[1], he had to give a tenth of the wood to the priest; should
he happen to get a second mowing of his meadow, tithe had to be
paid all over again; and the acorns he gathered in the woods or the
wild fruits he picked were all equally taxable. 'No matter what a
man's occupation was', wrote Dr J. R. H. Moorman, 'no matter
how he made his living nor how slender it was, the Church's net
was made with so fine a mesh that not even the smallest could
escape.'

As long as the medieval Church retained its power it steadily
enforced its demands on 'that which doth arise and grow by reason
and virtue of the ground'; on the 'increase of beasts, fishes and
fowls'; and on 'lawful and honest commodity obtained and pro-
cured by art, science and the manual occupation of some person'.
Rectors received the great tithes or those from corn, hay, and wood;
and the Vicars the rest of the predial tithes, plus all mixed and
personal tithes. There was little at first that the laity could do about
it; but from the fourteenth century onwards the storm began to
gather. Langland had suggested:

He that gave you your title should give you your wages
Or the Bishop that blesseth you if that ye be worthy.

John Ball was opposed to paying tithes to the richer clergy, when
the recipient was wealthier than the donor. John Wyclif and his
followers, the Lollards, objected to the payment of personal tithes
to non-residents; and advocated the then novel proposal that each
congregation should control its own priest and provide him with
a stipend.

[1] The statute, 45 Ed. III, c. 3, exempted the timber in the great
forests, which was of twenty years growth, from tithe, provided it was
sold for the owner's profit or used in the royal wars.

In the fifteenth century, following on the Black Death, there began a switch from corn-growing to pasture or an intensive agriculture, that was to continue through the next two centuries, accompanied by the introduction of new crops like hops, saffron, and tobacco. This was made possible by the practice of enclosure; but led to a series of disputes as to what was now titheable and what was not. The power of the clergy had been very greatly reduced by the Reformation; and they quickly found themselves fighting a losing battle to retain, let alone increase, the tithes they claimed to be due to them. They saw the common lands on which they had grazed their cattle and sheep, and the forest lands in which they had fed their swine and acquired timber for the repair of their houses and fuel for their fires, snatched from them and nothing given in return; since enclosed common lands and reclaimed lands were exempt from tithe.

Monastic and Crown property were also free from tithe; and the lay impropriators, who had acquired the former, together with their appropriated tithes, were bent on continuing the plunder of the Church that Henry VIII had begun. Large numbers of advowsons had fallen into their hands, and these they used as a weapon to extort economic concessions. Too often a presentation to a living was only made in exchange for some valuable quid pro quo, such as a lease of tithes or even of a whole benefice, a gift of glebe-land, a sale on advantageous terms, or perhaps an outright simoniacal contract involving a substantial money payment. The Lambeth Articles of 1561 threatened to deprive any parson who made such a compact; and the statutes of 13 Eliz. c.20. and 3 Car.I. c.5. forbade leases for more than three years, which would then only be valid as long as the incumbent was in residence. They also put a stop to the practice whereby a pension could be charged upon a benefice. None the less they were evaded; and all real attempts to curb the control of the squire over the parson failed; even those inaugurated by Archbishop Laud, and later by the Long Parliament. The dependence of the country clergy upon the squirearchy gradually became an established fact that has persisted right into modern times. It must be remembered, of course, that in the sixteenth, seventeenth, and eighteenth centuries a benefice was regarded more as a piece of property than a cure of souls, whose profits would come in whether the duties were performed or not.

The Puritans as the spiritual descendants of the Lollards were strongly opposed to pluralities, tithes, lay patronage, and lay impropriations. Furthermore they would have liked to have seen congregations choosing, controlling, and paying from voluntary subscriptions their own ministers. But they were never in a position fully to

implement such aims, even after the Long Parliament had won the
Civil War; for the simple reason that vested interests were always
too strong. There were, of course, plenty of lay patrons and lay
impropriators on the Roundhead side; while practical experience
quickly revealed that tithes were the easiest means of financing the
clergy, for which Parliament could find no workable alternative.
Pluralities alone were abolished for a time; and the parson was
warned:

> Bigamy of steeples is a hanging matter,
> Each must have one and curates will grow fatter.

However, they soon came creeping back again since the presbyterian Trustees for Maintenance, and later Cromwell himself, found
that the union of small parishes was essential if their incumbents
were to be provided with a living wage.

Despite the revolutionary changes brought about in all walks of
life during the hundred years that lay between the accession of
Queen Elizabeth and the Restoration of Charles II, the clergy had
never ceased to base their claim to tithe on the Divine Law, the
scriptural tenth; while at the same time strenuous efforts were made
on their behalf by the Bishops to secure the return of lay impropriations[1]. This led them into conflict with Parliament and the
Common Law courts, which championed the rights of the laity, and
asserted that tithes were only due where there was a legal as
opposed to a divine command to pay. The right to personal tithes
was in particular strenuously resisted and practically came to an end
with the passing of the statutes 2 and 3 Ed.VI.c.13., which freed
day labourers from all tithes on their wages; and further exempted
anyone who could not be proved to have paid them during the
preceding forty years. However, the clergy did not give in without
a fight; and isolated attempts to collect them were made even as late
as the beginning of the nineteenth century, when, as has already
been seen, Francis Lundy, Rector of Lockington in Yorkshire, had
a labourer imprisoned for failing to pay at the rate of 4d. in the
pound on his wages. The Rector of Clayworth, Notts., in 1683
tried to enforce a similar demand for a farthing in every shilling of
all servants' wages; but eventually dropped his claims after threatening lawsuits.

The introduction of the Commutation System or *modus deci-
mandi* at the beginning of the sixteenth century, added to the
parson's troubles. This simply meant that a rector or vicar
arrived at a legal arrangement with his tithe-payers, whereby in

[1] It was made more difficult because the bishops themselves were
impropriators.

return for a fixed annual payment, sometimes in cash but often still in kind, they were released from the normal ten per cent on their production. That was all very well as long as the value of money or the volume of production remained stable; but with a growing inflation, following in the footsteps of the upheavals of the Reformation and the influx of precious metals from the Americas, and more prosperous farming and trading, the parson found himself, like his modern successor, living on a small fixed income while prices soared. Frantic efforts, usually foiled by Parliament or the Common Law courts, were made by the Church either to get such commutations abolished altogether or else to have them revised in an upward direction. But commutation had come to stay, and eventually brought about the Commutation Act of 1836. The general effect was to create ill-feeling between the priest and his people, and the Ecclesiastical and Common Law courts.

The financial position of the clergy varied enormously, of course, in different parts of the country. In corn-growing areas, where there was still tithing in kind, rectors appeared comfortably off, judging from their wills and the inventories of their houses. On the other hand, those rectors or vicars who were trying to live on a grossly inadequate modus were often very badly hit. This applied particularly to incumbents who occupied impropriate livings, and were unable to persuade the impropriators to augment their incomes. Under Archbishop Laud an attempt was, indeed, made to compel impropriators to increase their vicars' salaries; but the success achieved, as for instance in the huge diocese of Lincoln, was very meagre.

Unfortunately every effort the parson himself made to defend and if possible increase, his income, notably his endeavours to tap the new sources of wealth of the clothiers, miners, graziers, and market gardeners, steadily increased an already strongly growing anti-clericalism. In particular the layman resented the parson's attempts to extend his tithing operations into the field of ferae naturae or that of the non-reproductive metals and minerals. The spiritual status of the priest had been seriously undermined by the Reformation. No longer did he hear confessions and absolve from guilt; no longer was he the indispensable mediator between God and Man. To the Puritan every man was now very largely his own priest, and the Bible had taken the place of the Church. Hence he bitterly resented paying tithes to a minister he did not want or like; and fees for ceremonies of which he did not approve. In some ways, in fact, the successful Puritan Revolution under the Long Parliament was a revolt against the economic policies of Laud and his Church as well as against those of Charles and the Crown.

At the Reformation, too, the parson had lost a great many little offerings and dues that he had previously received as a matter of course from his parishioners. These had consisted of congregational contributions at the four festivals of Christmas, Easter, the Festival and the Dedication of the Church; the mass pennies or small offerings of the faithful at the celebration of the Eucharist on Sundays, anniversaries, and trentals; the fees for the occasional offices; and collections taken from penitents making their confession. Certain oblations were also paid in cash or given in kind. There was the right of the priest to the loaves of bread and wax candles, which remained over from the Sunday services; a privilege that was sometimes abused. It was reported, for example, of Thomas Oxford, Vicar of Worminghall, in 1518, 'He will not suffer candles offered to the images of saints by parishioners to be lit, but straightway he takes them off and keeps them', in order, apparently, to light the Vicarage for nothing. Generous and grateful parishioners rewarded their incumbent from time to time with gifts of eggs, fowls, and other foods. Then, there were various perquisites to which the parson was entitled: mortuary dues were paid to him at each death in the village; a small legacy was given in return for the making and witnessing of a will; the sale or letting of seats in church—such as they were—were in his hands; and he was entitled to a number of tiny but vexatious taxes, like the plough penny exacted from each plough team in the parish or a small corn rent, which was payable at Martinmas. After the Reformation most of these were lost. All that remained were the surplice fees, Easter offerings, mortuaries, and the small payments for bread and wine made at Holy Communion or for the ringing of the church's bells at weddings and funerals. However, they still constituted a heavy burden on the poor, who resented them accordingly.

The income from the average medieval rectory had probably yielded about £10 per annum, which was a comfortable enough maintenance at the time, had it not been for the heavy out-goings of one kind or another that reduced its value by half. These included taxes to Rome in the form of first fruits and tenths, subsidies granted to the King, synodals and procurations due to the bishop or arch-deacon, the wages of assistant-curates and church officials, the upkeep of the chancel, poor relief, perhaps a pension to a pre-decessor, and the very considerable expense involved in the collection of the tithe itself. No wonder the medieval parson was often a poor man. In the reign of Queen Elizabeth the charges were certainly no lighter. First fruits and tenths were now payable to the Crown from all vicarages over £10 and from rectories over £7 in value. The clerical subsidies were fixed at the rate of six shillings in the pound; while in time of war the clergy had to contribute towards the provision of armour and munitions. Fees had still to be paid to the bishop at his visitation and to the archdeacon in his synod; but worst of all to the Royal Visitors, who, wrote William Harrison, 'doo commonlie visit the whole realme under the form of an ecclesiastical inquisition in which the clergy do usually paie double fees'. Finally, the incumbent was expected to be 'given to hospitality' and generous in poor relief. Furthermore, those of them whose benefices were worth more than £100 per annum in the Queen's Book had each to contribute £3 6s. 8d. annually towards the cost of maintaining poor scholars at the university. No wonder Harrison estimated: 'that of a benefice of twentie pounds by the yeare, the incumbent thinketh himselfe well acquitted if, all ordinary paiements being discharged, he may reserve thirteene pounds six shillings and eight pence towards his own sustentation and main-tenance of his familie.' By the seventeenth century the clerical subsidy had been reduced to 4s. in the pound; but this was offset by the fact that the clergy were now being subjected to heavy pressure in the matter of royal benevolences, which were enforced under threat of excommunication. The Archbishops could likewise claim a benevolence of one tenth from their clergy on the occasion of their installation.

For the first time, in the famous case of Ship Money, the parson was included in the national system of taxation; and whereas his separate taxation naturally disappeared during the Interregnum, it was finally surrendered after the Restoration, when in 1664 Claren-don and Archbishop Sheldon persuaded Convocation to give it up. About the same time the clergy also lost their claim to exemption from local taxation. They had been included for the poor rate in the Act of 1601; and the rest of their immunity, which had been swept away by the Commonwealth, was never restored. Henceforth the Church had to accept the principle that ministers like laymen were subject to all local taxation voted by Parliament, unless expressly excluded by statute.

The eviction of several thousand incumbents during the civil wars and under the Commonwealth and Protectorate, together with the intrusion of nonconformist ministers into their benefices, caused a further and violent disruption in the system of tithe pay-ments. Parliament had found itself obliged to continue that system; but many royalist parishioners refused to pay their tithes to the new intruded incumbent, raided the tithe barns, and secretly subsidized their ex-rector or vicar. The anti-clerical spirit abroad was no less hostile to the strait-laced Presbyterian than to the Romish Laudian; and often full advantage was taken of an obscure and chaotic situation to pay as little as possible to anyone at all. Parliament, through the Trustees for Maintenance, sought to augment the poorer livings with direct state grants, which were derived from the confiscated impropriations of the Church hierarchy and royalist gentry. Their aim was to bring all benefices up to a minimum income of £100; although this proved impossible without uniting some of the smaller parishes. And, as the rule of Oliver Cromwell and his Major Generals got into its stride, tithe-payments were as far as practicable strictly and regularly enforced. None the less when the King enjoyed his own again in 1660 a great deal of damage had been done to the economic structure of the Church in the country, from which it was slow to recover. State augmentations ceased; tithes on personal profits and wages had been permanently abandoned; other tithes could now be claimed only as a legal, and not as a divine right; all attempts to recover any appreciable amount of impropriated tithes had failed; and commutation contracts to the disadvantage of the clergy continued to be made. Meanwhile inflation showed no sign of ending. Ralph Josselin had written in September 1647: 'things are at that rate as never was in our days, wheat 8s, malt 4s, beefe 3d, butter 6½d, cheese 4d, candle 7d, currants 9d, sugar 18d and every other thing whatsoever deare'; while his contemporary, Henry Newcome, was equally concerned at the rising prices: 'We gave sixteen shillings a hoop for wheat, ten shillings for barley, between fifty shillings and three pounds for a load of malt, and so it put us behind for clothes.' These factors all contributed to the poverty of the country parson after the Restoration. Edward Chamberlayne, speaking about the social position of the parochial clergy in 1669, remarked sadly: 'At present the revenues of the English clergy are generally very small and insignificant'; and added: 'The great diminution of the revenues of the clergy, and the little care of augmenting and defending the patrimony of the Church, is the great reproach and shame of the English Reformation. . . . Men think it a stain to their blood to place their sons in that function; and women are ashamed to marry any of them.' However, some attempt had been made to augment the poorer vicarages. In a letter to the bishops in 1660 Charles II had exhorted them to provide a 'competent maintenance' for their own impropriate benefices and those of the deans and chapters; and by 1671 Eachard himself admitted that many bishops had augmented the vicarages in their gift. But it had all to be done on a voluntary basis, since Parliament steadily refused to pass any Act giving legal effect to Charles's letter.

The picture drawn by Macaulay in his famous *Third Chapter* is therefore substantially correct. Writing of the country parson in

1675 he declared: 'Often it was only by toiling on the glebe, by feeding swine, and by loading dung carts, that he could obtain daily bread; nor did his utmost exertions always prevent the bailiffs from taking his concordance and his inkstand in execution. It was a white day on which he was admitted into the kitchen of a great house, and regaled by the servants with cold meat and ale. His children were brought up like the children of the neighbouring peasantry. His boys followed the plough and his girls went out to service.' In these circumstances plurality was an economic necessity, which was recognized even by the most conscientious bishop. William Wake of Lincoln, for example, frankly admitted as much at the beginning of the eighteenth century. 'This I confess', he said, 'is a very melancholy, but withal a very just excuse, in many places.' Since the Reformation there had been a good deal of legislation seeking to control, regulate, and if possible reduce pluralities; but the steadily rising cost of living, together with the heavy taxation, defeated them all. For the clergy had somehow to make a living. The Canons of 1604 decreed that not more than two livings could be held by any one incumbent, who had to obtain a dispensation from residence and promise to supply a curate for the parish in which he did not live. Pluralities must also be within thirty miles of one another.

Another reason for the poverty of the clergy was to be found in the fact that there were too many of them. The shortage in Eliza-bethan times had given place, from the seventeenth century onwards, to a remarkable surplus; and the Universities were now turning out clerics at an alarming rate. Large numbers of these men, as Eachard truly pointed out in *The Grounds and Occasions of the Clergy and Religion Enquired Into*, were ordained on the strength of fictitious titles and had no real jobs awaiting them. Others became an easy prey for the rapacious pluralist, who haggled with them until he had found a curate 'who', as William Jones, curate of Broxbourne, bitterly remarked, 'will starve with the fewest symptoms of discontent'. A return compiled for the benefit of the Governors of Queen Anne's Bounty in 1704/5 and published in 1711 disclosed that out of some 9,180 livings paying first fruits and tenths: 5,082 were worth less than £80; 3,826 less than £50; and 1,216 less than £20. The Bounty itself was founded in 1704 by an Act of Parliament, 2 and 3 Anne c. II., that empowered the Queen to form a corporation by royal charter on which was settled the whole revenue from the first fruits and tenths. Furthermore any charitable person, who so desired, might now 'by deed or will give to the Corporation lands, tenements, and hereditaments, goods and chattels, towards the augmentation of the clergy.' The corporation could also make purchases without licence in mortmain. At the same time by another Act, 5 and 6 Anne c.27., all livings under £50 in value were exempted from first fruits and tenths, numbering nearly 4,000 parishes out of a total of 10,000. However, for the next decade the governors had little or no money to spare for the direct augmentation of benefices, since their revenues were swallowed up by the pensions that had been originally imposed upon the fund by Charles II in order to maintain his royal favourites; and which accounted for some £10,950 out of a total sum of £17,000. There was, too, considerable difficulty in collecting arrears, especially from bishops and other church dignitaries; while the method of collecting itself —the Exchequer being responsibe for the tenths and the bishops for the first fruits—was slow, antiquated, and inefficient.

But by 1714 most of the teething troubles had been overcome; and augmentaions began in real earnest. In the second charter of that year certain fundamental rulings were laid down. These declared that augmentation must always be by purchase of land and not by pension; that £200 grants would be made to meet equal benefactions; and that the rest of the available money, also in £200 grants, should be allocated by lot to benefices under £10 nominal value. By 1737 whig hostility to the Church had borne fruit in legislation that largely put an end to benefactions—they were forbidden by an Act, 9.Geo.II.c.36.—and for the rest of the century the governors' grants had to be made by the less satisfactory method of casting lots. Fortunately these restrictions were removed in 1803 by another Act, Geo.III.c.107., with the pleasing result that augmentation by benefaction rather than by lottery became the accepted norm once more. The success of Queen Anne's Bounty could not be denied; yet other suggestions for the state augmentation of benefices fell on deaf ears. There was, for example, Robert Nelson's plea contained in his *Address to Persons of Quality and Estate*, and published in 1715. This put forward a plan whereby the Government would introduce a tax, which would be used to buy out lay impropriators, restore their tithes to the Church, and thus eradicate 'a national sin'.

The Bounty itself would certainly have been more effective if there could have been a revaluation and redistribution of benefice incomes; but a scheme to this effect, which was debated by the House of Commons in 1837, came to nothing. But by that date the Ecclesiastical Commissioners had been appointed, who immediately set to work to try to augment the poorer livings up to a fixed minimum out of their 'unhallowed spoils', derived from the endowments of bishoprics and dignities. By 1843 they were prepared, if possible, to adopt the following scale: Parishes, whose population was over 2,000, would receive from all sources a minimum income of £150; 1,000, £120; 500, £100; below 500, £80. In every case, however, the patronage had to be 'public', i.e. non-saleable. The extension of the scheme to private patronage livings depended upon a promise of a two-thirds benefaction. Unfortunately the Commissioners' means proved quite inadequate to meet their liabilities; and in 1844 they had to suspend augmentation altogether. It was not revived on any large scale until the end of the century.

William Cobbett had estimated that some 1,496 parishes were in the hands of only 332 incumbents; and even the Ecclesiastical Commissioners were reluctantly forced to the conclusion that plurality in the case of very poor benefices was still an economic necessity. But by the Pluralities Act of 1838, 2.Vict.c.106., the thirty mile limit was reduced to ten; and in 1885 was further reduced to four, which was to be calculated by road instead of by how the crow flies.

The country parson had always had his glebe farm; which was originally worked solely as a means of supporting himself and his family. At first the system of enclosure hit him hard, since even if he enclosed himself he did not possess the necessary capital to improve his land; and by the Act 21.Hen.VIII.c.13. he was forbidden to lease lands for farming purposes. He was, in fact, prohibited from buying or selling anything for profit, whether corn, cattle, or merchandise; and it was not until 1805 that another Act allowed him to do so. Henceforth parsons could become large farmers or even bankers or brokers. Already during the eighteenth century the energetic, knowledgeable and enterprising farming parson had been able to do much with his own glebe. Aided by his wife, who was often herself the daughter of a farmer, and by stalwart sons and daughters, the rector found that by enclosing he could take full advantage of the revolution in agricultural methods, the introduction of new crops, and the improved breeds of sheep and cattle. Consequently his profits steadily increased. The story of the archdeacon who found a country churchyard growing wheat and warned the incumbent, 'This must not occur again'; but was promptly met with the retort, 'Certainly not, it will be barley next year', may well have applied to this type of go-ahead clerical farmer. When, too, the squire's younger son began to take over the family living he brought capital with him to improve both land and buildings. This was a period of artificially cheap labour costs, and a parson with a business head, like John Leroo of Long Melford in Suffolk, found it a profitable business to rent his land to tenants. By judiciously raising the rents of this glebe and the composition for his tithes, Leroo increased the total income of his living from

£528 4s. 6d. in 1791 to £1,219 15s. od. in 1817; and when he died in 1819 the advowson was sold for £15,000. These were the years, of course, of the high price of corn, safeguarded by protection, which in 1800 reached the record figure for wheat of 127s. a quarter.

As more and more glebe farms were leased to tenants and tithes commuted for fixed money payments the personal interest of the parson in the land began to wane, and the farmers came to resent a sleeping partner, who risked no capital, but exacted his pound of flesh in bad years as well as good ones. The cash they handed over at the annual audit dinner was no less grudgingly paid than the tenth sheaf or the tenth pig in days gone by. In the early years of the nineteenth century Arthur Young had spoken of 'the horrid greediness' of the clergy for tithes, which, he declared, was 'the disgrace of England'. But there was another side to the picture. The clergy had to pay a very heavy land tax, rates, an inflated poor rate, and the expenses of collection, all out of their own pockets. None the less in one respect at least their position had improved: Tithes could now be charged on reclaimed land, provided it was not proved to be barren. Often, indeed, the parson was only too glad to accept a rate-free composition at a greatly reduced figure, in view of the uneconomic Speenhamland system that had been introduced into the Home Counties in 1795. However, with the advent of the Victorian Age clerical economics took a decided change for the better. In the first place the disastrous inflationary spiral was reduced to a healthy normality; and the cost of living at long last became relatively stable. In the second, the highly successful Tithe Commutation Act of 1836, which established money payments on a legal and satisfactory basis, brought a much needed measure of peace to the relations between parson and farmer. By this Act the value of tithes was assessed on the basis of the average value of all tithes over the last seven years; while the tithe-owner remained responsible for paying his own rates. But in order to make its purchasing power in the future correspond to prices, the value was tied to that of the three principal cereals over a period of seven years. Finally, it must be remembered that the parson himself was now being drawn more and more from the higher classes in the community, often possessed a private income of his own, and had, therefore, no longer any real incentive—it would have been below his dignity— to grasp at every penny and start legal proceedings over his tithes at the slightest provocation.

The repeal of the Corn Laws in 1846 did not really make its effect felt upon agriculturalists until the late 'seventies; but then trouble started up again in real earnest. From 1883 until 1918 the tithe-rent charge declined annually; but even so it was a heavy burden on the farmers, who demanded concessions from the clergy that they were unwilling to grant. Many parsons employed lawyers for the recovery of their tithes; and this, naturally, did not increase their popularity with their parishioners. The Tithe Act of 1891, however, not only gave a welcome relief to the tithe-payer, but shifted the burden from the tenant to the landowner, who was usually also the squire. So where parson and squire were on good terms, and the latter was a wealthy and generous patron, all went well. But, alas, in numerous cases the squire was no friendlier than the farmer, and a great deal more powerful. The parson was not always to blame. Well-to-do clergy with private means were never in a majority. There were all too many poor incumbents, who were financially very hard hit at this time. So much so that certain dioceses, notably Lincoln, were compelled to formulate their own schemes for augmenting the stipends of poorly endowed benefices. Another Tithe Act of 1899 remitted half the rates payable by the clerical tithe-owners on their tithes, making the Inland Revenue responsible for the remainder. Furthermore the redemption of tithes, that had been achieved on a wholesale basis in Ireland at the time of the Church's disestablishment, was encouraged over here on the principle that the annual income from government securities should equal the amount previously received from tithe. Fortunately, too, the Church Commissioners were by 1908 in a sufficiently strong financial position to maintain the minimum benefice income at £150 per annum.

Farming once again became prosperous during and after the first world war, when a great many tenant farmers bought their land from the squire. And the cry was immediately raised that tithe-owners should not be allowed to share in these increased profits. Pressure was brought to bear upon the Government; and an Act was passed in 1918 fixing tithe at its then existing level for the next eight years. But the farmers had no intention of allowing tithe-payments to rise when this period had expired; so they formed themselves into tithe-payers' associations, which agitated in season and out of season against that part of the 1918 Act which decreed that after 1926 tithe should be valued on a fifteen year average of the price of the three main cereals. As usual the laity had their way, and the Tithe Act of 1925 stabilized tithe for the next eighty-five years; while at the same time authorizing its collection through Queen Anne's Bounty Office. The only advantages accruing from these sorry proceedings, as far as the clergy were concerned, were that the unpleasant business of collecting was now taken out of their hands, and that they no longer had to pay their share of its rateable value, which devolved upon the general body of rate-payers, provided the benefice income in each case did not exceed £300. About the same time the Church Commissioners were able to raise the minimum stipend of most benefices from £150 to £350 per annum.

But none of these concessions permanently satisfied the farmers, who began their agitation once again as soon as post-war farming ran into the doldrums. The charges of greediness, laziness, and incompetence were freely levelled against the clerical fraternity. Robertson Scott wrote in *England's Green and Pleasant Land*, which was first published in 1925: 'In the fireside judgement of the mass of the agricultural labouring families, the average parson is witless and lazy, a self-satisfied drone, who, by the advantage of his social position, has secured a soft job, to which he hangs on, although he knows, or ought to know, that much of what he keeps on saying about the gravest matters that can engross the human mind is untrue.' This was a savage indictment that many countrymen would have echoed during the stormy years that led up to the Tithe Redemption Act of 1936. Queen Anne's Bounty Office certainly faced a hard task in collecting tithe-rents during the lean years of the early 'thirties. Yet they had to do their duty by the clergy; while showing as much mercy and consideration as they possibly could where they found genuine hardship. In some parts of the country the farmers launched a campaign of refusing to pay, which inevitably led on to forced sales and distraint. I was myself a curate at this time in a Kent village; and can well recall the bitter comments passed in public houses; the boards stuck up outside church doors, so that the departing congregations could read such words as: 'The Church's One Foundation, Tithe'; and the effigies of Queen Anne and the Archbishop of Canterbury burnt before excited crowds of countrymen. The matter was probably made worse by the fact that the farmer was dealing with an impersonal body, of which it might unkindly have been said; 'It had no heart to be touched and no bottom to be kicked'; whereas in the past the personal and informal contacts he had formed with his own parson could and did frequently result in some agreed and friendly solution.

Undoubtedly the divorce of the parson from the land had developed at an alarming rate. Since 1918 'redemption', encouraged by simplified legislation, had been gathering volume and momentum; and ultimately this was the solution arrived at. By the Tithe Redemption Act of 1936, which satisfied the farmers but sadly crippled the Church in the country, all future tithe payments were to be made to the Government instead of to the benefice. In return the Government issued tithe stock, which represented about seventy-five per cent of its former value; while at the same time undertook to safeguard the interests of sitting incumbents. At the next vacancy, however, each benefice lost something like twenty-five per cent of its former tithe income. How many millions of pounds these successive Tithe Acts have cost the Church it would be hard to estimate; and whether the relative peace they have brought to the countryside is worth the sacrifice, remains a more than open question.

There have, of course, been many factors that helped to worsen the position of the country clergy since 1936, notably the inflationary spiral that grew up after the second world war; but never the less tithe redemption was one of the principal causes behind the regrettable Pastoral Re-organization Measure of 1949. Meanwhile the Ecclesiastical Commissioners, as far as lay in their power, had proceeded with their schemes of augmentation; and it has, indeed, been estimated that between 1840 and 1935 some 9,300 benefices were endowed by them at an annual cost of £1,828,000. But by 1943 it had become obvious that something more was still needed, and there began those ever more frantic appeals to the laity to increase their quota contributions, as the only available means whereby incumbents can receive anything approaching a minimum living stipend. The following table, giving the sources of the incomes of the parochial clergy for 1953, clearly reveals the extremely important part played by the 'new money' which is raised in the parishes:

### Stipends of the Parochial Clergy in 1953

1. From the Church Commissioners for incumbents    £6,013,697
   From the Church Commissioners for curates    £ 391,800

   Total    £6,405,497

2. From the parishes for incumbents    £1,224,015
   From the parishes for curates    £ 766,645

   Total    £1,990,660

Tithe has gone, but glebe remains. The President of Jesus College, Cambridge, writing in the October, 1953, number of *Church and Countryside*, and again in the January, 1957, number of *Parson and Parish*, deplored what he called, 'the voluntary disestablishment of the Church'. There was today, he declared, little difficulty about selling glebe; for farmers were able and anxious to buy land, and diocesan authorities were encouraging sales. A hard-pressed incumbent, faced by heavy dilapidations, might yet hesitate to raise the rent of a tenant, who was also a parishioner and possibly even a churchwarden. How much better then, from the short-term point of view, to sell for a good price and invest the money in government stock. He could well argue that the fate of his successor was no concern of his. But from the long-term standpoint such a policy is disastrous; since the purchasing power of money is steadily declining, while land and buildings always retain their value. As wages and costs rise, so will rents and 'many a farm which was rented at £100 a year a century ago is rented now at twice that sum, and the tenant does not complain'. With the lifting of the Rent Restriction Acts house rents will rise too. 'What', asked Mr Gardner-Smith, 'will be the position of the parson a hundred years hence who has to live on annuities purchased in 1957?' His own solution, and one that is much canvassed in certain quarters, is that each diocese should set up a central office, staffed by a qualified land-agent and his assistants, which would take charge of all the glebe, apart from gardens and paddocks adjoining the house, collect the rents, and pay them to the individual incumbents concerned. Another suggestion is that the Church Commissioners might take over all the glebe-lands, pay the incumbents at an agreed rate, and make what profit they could for their funds above and beyond that figure. As I write the whole matter is very much in the melting pot; but in any case it appears that the country parson's last links with the soil are about to be severed at any moment; and he is likely to become more and more dependent upon his parishioners for his livelihood. Perhaps the day is not far distant when the old Leveller and Quaker ideals will be realized of parishes choosing and paying their own ministers, and thus achieving a true congregational democracy.

Despite all the centuries-old frictions and disputes occasioned between the clergy and their people in the collection of tithes or the raising of rents, the close association of the parson with the soil has in the past provided a deep and close bond uniting him with his parishioners. At first as a peasant himself he laboured alongside them in the open field; and even when at a later date he was concerned with the land merely as the receiver of the tithes and the landlord of the glebe farm, yet he could always rejoice with them in a successful season, when all would share in its fruits and profits, and sorrow at a bad harvest in which all again would suffer. It behoved him, then, to be something of an expert in weather lore and crop rotation and the breeding of cattle, sheep, and pigs; in the repair of the farm-house, the amenities of the farmyard, and the state of the labourers' cottages. Here was an endless source for sermon-making and catechizing; for informal talk, and gossip in home or ale-house. Farming and gardening were in the country priest's blood, just as much as in that of his flock; and in such labours he was enabled to bring them all closer to the Divine Creator.

Oh Adam was a gardener, and God who made him sees,
That half a proper gardener's work is done upon his knees.

# CHAPTER VIII

# The Evolution of the Parsonage

THE ORIGINAL PARSONAGE house was a very simple affair consisting of a small one- or two-roomed timber-framed shanty, filled in with wattles and clay and roofed over with thatch or shingles. Some better class rectors might inhabit more commodious dwellings built on the lines of a manor house. These last would contain a principal hall with annexes at either end. The hall itself, with its high-ceilinged roof, small unglazed windows far from the ground, and great stone hearth at its centre, was the principal living-room, where the inmates lived, ate, slept, and cooked; although the annex at the lower end might occasionally boast a kitchen as well as a brew-house and buttery. The upper annex, on the other hand, usually consisted of a two-storeyed building, whose ground floor contained stores of all sorts; while the first storey, known as the great chamber, could be utilized as a guest house. This 'solar' might, indeed, be quite comfortably furnished with stools, oak chests, and window seats; possibly even with a spinning wheel.

As the Middle Ages went on superior rectories of that type began to be constructed of stone instead of wood, a good example of which can still be seen at West Dean in Sussex. This is a late thirteenth-century house with traced windows and a newel staircase. Remains of many of these better class parsonages are not uncommon: sometimes lying in ruins, sometimes extensively restored, like an early sixteenth-century rectory at Easton-on-the-Hill in Northamptonshire, which is now used as a farm building, and sometimes disguised by modern additions as at Warmington in the same county. Occasionally they are preserved as places of historical importance; of which Alfriston Vicarage in Sussex is an outstanding instance. From the thirteenth century onwards these parsonages undoubtedly became more elaborate and comfortable, with additional guest and servant quarters; whilst the high roof of the hall was often converted into a sleeping loft. But when viewing such surviving types, it must not be forgotten that the poorer vicars and *capellani* were housed under far more wretched conditions. It was customary for their small hovels to stand in or near the churchyard, so that their parishioners could find them at or close by the church in an emer-

A medieval rectory at Easton-on-the-Hill, Northamptonshire, now used as a farm building.

The Elizabethan vicarage at Sleaford, Lincolnshire. The sixteenth-century porch, surmounted by a cross, is at the left.

The sixteenth-century rectory at Aldwincle, Northamptonshire,
birthplace of the poet Dryden.

Blatherwycke Rectory, Northamptonshire, a substantial house of the
seventeenth and eighteenth centuries.

gency. Occasionally a dwelling-house was actually attached to the west end of the church itself; or a small portion of its interior walled off to provide the resident priest with a tiny home. At Radwinter in Essex there are still two existing buildings known as the 'Lesser' and 'Greater' Vicarage. These might have housed respectively the assistant clergy and the incumbent.

The poor vicar at any rate had the right to 'husbote' or free wood from the forest for building and maintaining his vicarage; but the cost of repairs and replacements, particularly to jerry-built huts liable to constant destruction by storm or fire, must have been extremely heavy. Each parsonage, too, would own a number of farm out-buildings for keeping cattle, sheep, and pigs, besides the traditional tithe barn. The duty of the clergy, moreover, to be 'given to hospitality', especially if situated on or near any of the main roads, necessitated the erection of ample stabling for horses. At Kingston-on-Thames, for instance, the vicar possessed 'a stable for six horses, all covered with tiles'. Consequently dilapidations, which until quite modern times were a charge on the out-going incumbent, might be assessed, even in pre-Reformation days, at as much as £20.

The incumbent did not live alone. He was officially celibate; but this state of virginity was not always strictly observed. Writing of the visitations in the diocese of Lincoln from 1517 to 1531, Professor Hamilton Thompson said: 'The presence of women in rectory and vicarage houses was in some districts a subject of common enquiry; it was seldom censured, and as often as not the churchwardens stated that there was no cause for suspicion or objection.' In many cases these may have been female relations or servants, but not invariably. There were the *uxorati* or openly married clergy; others who, although nominally unmarried, lived faithfully with one consort all their lives; and finally those who were frankly promiscuous and unable to resist temptation when visiting their spiritual daughters. The curate of Henley-on-Thames, for example, in 1530 actually had the audacity to refer to the child of his 'spiritual daughter' as his 'spiritual son'! Consequently female inhabitants of medieval parsonages were not uncommon. However, besides his unofficial family an incumbent was expected to house an official staff of perhaps as many as four or five assistants, even in a small village. These were the men who helped him to run a straggling country parish with its outlying hamlets.

Furniture was usually scarce and simple. The better-class house could boast of trestle tables, benches, and stools, and possibly tapestries or painted cloths on the walls. Pewter dishes, horn drinking cups, water pots, iron cooking vessels, and other apparatus might be found in the kitchen; while vats and tubs for brewing pur-

I

poses usually existed in the brewhouse. But when your house was liable to be broken into, blown down, or set on fire at any moment, a superfluity of household goods would have been an embarrassment. Sir Richard Brone, Rector of Harston in Leicestershire, who died in 1519, left household goods worth but fifteen shillings and fivepence. His furniture consisted of 'three bordes', one chair, a pair of tongs, and a brand iron, two cooking pots, a pan and four pieces of pewter for eating purposes, three pairs of sheets, a pair of rough blankets, and a 'beyde Cower'. No bedstead is mentioned in his inventory; so he probably slept on one of the 'bordes'.

By the middle of the sixteenth century life was not only more secure, but standards of living had risen appreciably; and these facts became mirrored in the later Tudor parsonages. Sir Henry Burtby of Little Stretton, who died only twenty years later than his neighbour of Harston, was certainly much more comfortably placed. 'Unlike the comfortless Rector of Harston', wrote W. G. Hoskins, 'eating off bare boards by rushlight, the parson of Little Stretton supped off a folding-table covered with a linen tablecloth which bore two candlesticks for light.' His house, too, was bigger, and contained a third room, a kitchen, as well as the more normal hall and parlour. Parson Pecocke of Hatton in Lincolnshire about the same date was in possession of an exceptionally lordly rectory for the period. This consisted of a hall, parlour, inner and outer chambers, a sleeping loft over the hall, a second parlour, a larder, a bolting house and cheese chamber, besides many out-buildings, including a beast house, malt house, and wool house. The learned Matthew Knyghtley, Rector of Cossington, who died in 1561, dwelt in a parsonage that contained at least three bedrooms, which were furnished with down or feather beds. The best type of Elizabethan parsonage was even more imposing, and began to ape the proportions of a manor house. William Rustat of Barrow-on-Soar in the year of the Armada inhabited a Vicarage of some fourteen rooms of one kind and another; while the Lincolnshire rectory of Thorpe-on-the-Hill towards the close of the reign ran to sixteen separate apartments. One at Little Bromley in Essex early in the seventeenth century was described as follows:

> A large parsonage house compass'd with a mote, a gatehouse, with a large orchard and a little garden all within the mote, which together with the circuit of the house, contains about half an acre of ground; and without the mote there is a yard in which there is another gate-house, and a stable, and a hay-house adjoining, also a barn of twenty-five yards long, and nine yards wide, and about seventy-nine and a half acres of glebe land.

A few of these moats remain. There is one encircling part of old Haughton Rectory in Staffordshire. 'The rectory moat is always dry now', wrote T. F. Royds, the present patron of the living; and added that the rectory site was probably originally the seat of the lord of the manor, who built the church. 'I was talking to a parson recently', recorded Kathleen Jarvis in her *Impressions of a Parson's Wife*, published in 1950, 'who had been offered a living in a country area. He had just returned from inspecting the parish and the rectory. There was a moat, he said, there were vast areas of pleasure garden, and a vast number of lawns, each large enough to take the proverbial battleship.' No doubt the pleasure gardens and lawns were the products of Victorian England, but the moat must have originated in a rougher and tougher age.

But to return. By the end of the sixteenth century fashions in architecture were changing; and the importance of the hall had dwindled. In some instances it was now no more than an entry or porch. On the other hand, as Elizabethan inventories of parsonage houses go to show, provision had to be made for such innovations as stair-heads and stair-chambers, a study, and a maid's room. The parson's study had become a necessity, due to the Elizabethan drive to raise the educational standards of the clergy; and repeated references to resident maidservants went to prove that the old spartan regime of the 'prestes boy' had vanished, if not for ever, yet for centuries to come. Matthew Knyghtley's Rectory, for example, was run by a day-woman, two servants, and a cook. But Elizabethan parsonages not only possessed additional rooms, they were also very much more comfortably furnished. Up to the middle of the sixteenth century the necessities of life and labour had continued to loom disproportionately large. Coarse bedding, pots and pans, agricultural tools, brewing apparatus, sacks of grain, cheeses and butter, wool and salted meat, might be found in great profusion; but chairs, forms, tables, carpets, cushions, and even beds were often conspicuous by their absence. Now the framed table was ousting trestles and boards; while chairs and window-seats, containing cushions, were displacing stools and forms. Stained-glass windows, carpets, tester-beds, arrases, and painted cloths were making their appearance in the richer type of parsonage, where the rectorial bed, a magnificent four-poster, equipped with hangings and a feather mattress, was sometimes valued at several pounds. The medieval priest rarely possessed a book, even the Bible; and could boast of but few clothes, valuables, or other personal belongings. Hooker's contemporaries, however, often owned considerable libraries, besides quantities of clothes and plate, including silver ware. Mr Fisher, Rector of Bassingham in Lincolnshire, bequeathed to his heirs a wardrobe consisting of four gowns (two furred and two lined), three jackets of camlet and two others of cloth, three pairs of hose, two tippets of velvet and another of cloth, all of which were valued at £4 2s. od. He also left behind him a considerable quantity of pewter vessels. Roger Routh of Hellawe in the same county owned, in addition to his pewter, six silver spoons, which were valued at £3. Matthew Knyghtley likewise had three silver spoons, but his were only worth twelve shillings. His books, however, were priced at £20. The studious Elizabethan parson might own a library running to a hundred volumes or more. These were usually housed in the study, which would also normally contain a table, chair, and bed. For books in the sixteenth century were far too rare and valuable to rank merely as ornaments. They would be studied deep into the night, and probably early in the morning as well.

The advent of the parson's wife and maidservants added considerably to the comfort and amenities of the rectory. And even the poorer vicarages began to stock quantities of sheets, cloths, coverlets, and towels, improved cooking utensils, and such items of female industry as the spinning wheel and the loom. As yet the parson's wife was barely tolerated, and played but little part in the life of the village. Many unkind things were said about her. Mr and Mrs Holland of King's Sutton in Northamptonshire actually declared in June 1610 that, 'the World was never merrie since priests wear married'; and remarked of their own vicar's wife: 'The first night she was married to him gave hir selffe to the divell.' Her principal function, in fact, was to produce children, which she did so readily that some country clergy found it difficult to keep their heads above the financial waters.

The Vicar of Cosby in Leicestershire wrote in 1614: 'my living is verie small about xli communibus annis my charge verie great xiii children livinge and I live in debt.' His neighbour at Hungerton was in the same predicament: 'My livinge is verie small . . . if I had not lately received a gratuity from the rest of the brethren I had not been able to have maintayned myselfe and eight children till this tyme.' When these children were grown it was a different story; for then they could be most profitably employed on the glebe. George Herbert's *Country Parson* made choice of his wife, 'rather by his ear, than by his eye; his judgement, not his affection, found out a fit wife for him, whose humble and liberal disposition he preferreth before beauty or honour'. Then, having chosen her, 'he gives her respect both afore her servants, and others, and half at least of the government of the house', but 'never so giving over the reins, but that he sometimes looks how things go, demanding an account.' At Bemerton in Wiltshire, Herbert's own wife was allowed to play the lady bountiful in the village, but without giving herself any airs. Her husband warned her: 'You are now a minister's wife, and must now so far forget your father's house, as not to claim a precedence of any of your parishioners; for you are to know, that a priest's wife can challenge no precedence or place, but that which she purchases by her obliging humility, and I am sure, places so purchased do best become them.' The Herberts built their own parsonage out of their own pockets. Engraved over the mantelpiece in the principal room, still the hall, were the following lines:

> To My Successor.
> If thou chance for to find
> A new house to thy mind,
> And built without thy cost;
> Be good to the poor
> As God gives thee store,
> And then my labour's not lost.

Other parsons were not averse from leaving their mark behind them. The Revd D. L. Scott, the present Rector of Rippingale, wrote to me in July, 1957: 'Recently I happened to be at Leadenham, which has a very pleasing rectory, probably of the William and Mary period. Built onto it is a later wing over the doorway of which this much earlier inscription has been preserved:

> Misericordias Domini
> In Arterna Canabo [sic]
> Iohannes Dee
> 1561.'

John Dee, the astrologer, although Rector of Leadenham at this date never actually resided in the parish.

Despite all the increased comfort and new building to be found in the richer seventeenth-century parsonages, there still remained many small, poor houses built on the old conventional lines. At Broadwindsor the historian William Fuller inhabited a cottage; while the bachelor poet, Robert Herrick, described his home at Dean Prior in Devon in the following happy terms:

> Lord Thou hast given me a cell
> Wherein to dwell
> A little house whose humble roof
> Is weather proof;
> Under the spars of which I lie
> Both soft and dry.
>
> . . .

> Like as my parlour, so my Hall
> And kitchen's small
> A little buttery and therein
> A little bin,
> Which keeps my little loaf of bread
> Unchipt, unflead;
> Some brittle sticks of thorn or briar
> Make me a fire,
> Close by whose living coal I sit
> And glow like it.

Seventeenth-century clerical wills and inventories provide us with some interesting examples of the type of house now inhabited by the well-to-do country clergy. Here are two taken at random from a wide selection: The Reverend Martin Ballard, who was Vicar of Upton-near-Southwell for thirty-six years and survived the Commonwealth and Protectorate, died in March 1663/4. His last will and testament, which was dictated to his son-in-law the day before his death, informs us that his vicarage, constructed, apparently, on conventional lines, contained six rooms and a dairy, namely: 'Ye house', or principal hall, 'ye parlour', 'ye little parlour', 'ye chamber', 'ye kitchen', 'ye studie', and 'ye butterie', or dairy. The hall, the only room in the house that possessed a fireplace, was the dining-room and also the place where most of the cooking was done, since it boasted a formidable array of fire-irons, including tongs, shovel, spit, and cob-irons. The parlour, which was the vicar's bed-sitting-room, was a great deal more comfortable. But the chamber, the big upstairs apartment, was simply a store-house filled with farm implements, wheat, and pease. The contents of the vicarage were impressive. There were, to begin with, all the latest comforts: framed tables, a four-poster bed with a wooden ceiling, cupboards and presses, a number of chairs, 'one feather bed', 'one little deske', 'five interior doors', canvas cloths painted to look like tapestry, and a warming-pan, besides an abundance of such things as bedding, cooking utensils, and plate. In the study there was a library worth 15s.; while the Vicar's 'purse and aparell' were valued at £1 6s. 8d.

The Reverend Isaac Allen, Rector of Prestwick, was ousted from his living and all his goods sequestrated in 1645. 'An inventorie of the goods and chatteles of Isaak Allen', taken on 30 October of that year, give an excellent account of his rectory and its furnishings. Here was a fine rectory, indeed, with twenty-two rooms, excluding outhouses, but including others like cellars, brewhouse, day-house, cheese chamber, larder, and closet, that were simply store-rooms. The traditional hall with its parlours (three in this case), great

chamber, and kitchen quarters still constituted the bulk of the house.
But in addition there were the by now fairly normal study and
maid's chamber, and some elaborate rooms known as 'the hanging
chamber', 'yellow chamber', 'chappell chamber', and 'brushing
chamber', besides a servants' bedroom for male retainers. The contents were abundant and valued at as much as £96 19s. 10d. The
actual household stuff included 'field' chairs, framed tables, buffet-
stools, court cupboards, beds and bedding, curtains, linen, plate,
kitchen gear, and brewing apparatus. Each room was well filled.
Even the maids' chamber had 'three little beds with furniture for
two'; and several of the principal bedrooms boasted canopied beds
with curtains. The study contained one hundred and fifty books,
and one chair; while the hall possessed as many as three tables, five
chairs, and five cushions.

Much damage was done to the parsonages during the Civil Wars.
Some were gallantly defended by their owners and had to be taken
by storm. Others were wantonly looted and set on fire. But it was
not always the Roundheads who were the aggressors. John Dod,
Vicar of Fawsley in Northamptonshire, was plundered three times
by the Cavaliers. At their second arrival he was ill in bed, but that
did not prevent them from cutting away his bed-curtains and
stealing the pillows from under his head. On the third occasion he
sat by his parlour fire and watched them ransack the house. When,
however, one of the plunderers carried down the sheets from his
bedroom, deposited them near the Vicar and then went in search of
further loot, Dod promptly concealed the best pair under the
cushion on which he sat and thus, as he chuckled to himself afterwards, 'plundered the plunderers'.

A number of intruded ministers, who had occupied the parsonage
after the sequestration of the living, were, particularly in 1657,
attacked in their turn by royalist mobs, often headed by the ex-
rector himself or his sons, and their homes seized or wrecked. At
North Kilworth in Leicestershire the dispossessed Rector, Samuel
Cotton, supported by some Cavaliers, threw his Presbyterian
successor and his wife out into the street, and held the house for
some time against all comers. The puritanical Ralph Josselin, Vicar
of Earls Colne, recorded in his diary how in June 1648 the royalists
plundered the town and the vicarage: 'On Monday morning', he
wrote, 'the enemy came to Colne, were resisted by our towne men.
No part of Essex gave them so much opposition as wee did; they
plundered us and mee in particular, of all that was portable, except
brasse, pewter and bedding'.

In any case few repairs were carried out during these troublesome
years; and very little new building was undertaken. Consequently

at the Restoration most clerical homes were in a sadly dilapidated state, from which they were slow to recover. Most episcopal and archidecanal visitations of this period disclosed numbers of dilapidated, tumbledown, or non-existent parsonages; and even as late as 1702 Church Honeybourne in Worcestershire reported: 'Rector's house burnt in the wars', which had evidently never been replaced. Macaulay did not greatly exaggerate when in his description of the country parson in 1675 he referred to the holes appearing more and more plainly in the thatch of his parsonage. For, despite the examples of better-class seventeenth-century rectories that have survived, it has to be remembered that the bulk of the country clergy still dwelt in small, low, thatched houses, little better than glorified cottages, which contained as a rule a considerable number of farm outbuildings. Writing about one such vicarage at Thorpe in Yorkshire in 1703 a correspondent informed the Archbishop of York: 'There may be a parlour, a hall, and a kitchen with a chimney in every one; also a pantry and three chambers over all . . . the outhouse is a stable.' This was, indeed, typical of the snug little vicarage of the period.

The Curate of Lund, also in Yorkshire, depicted a similar compact parsonage in 1763: 'The Parsonage and Dove Coat', he wrote to a prospective buyer of the advowson, 'are of brick not long since built, with sufficient Barn room and other conveniences, a small orchard and Garth, which is all the enclosed grassing belonging to it, and five oxgangs of glebe land.' But the trouble lay in the fact that there were not enough of them to go round; and not sufficient money forthcoming to build others. A good example of the kind of situation existing in the parishes is provided at Cumberworth, yet another Yorkshire living, where in 1705 the 'Minister's house was ruined and irreparable'. It was, therefore, decided by the patron to keep the benefice vacant until, with the assistance of the parishioners, enough funds had been accumulated to build a rectory and so 'encouraged a good man to accept the poor donative'. Eventually a beginning was made by erecting the frame-work of the house at a cost of £39 10s. od.; but here 'the work rested', since the parishioners, who had promised so much, 'have performed nothing'. Accordingly the Archbishop was sadly informed that after all 'the next incumbent must be at the expense of finishing it'; an unhappy position that might well daunt 'a good man'.

Yet even where a house already existed it was often extremely dilapidated; and the incoming incumbent usually encountered the greatest difficulty in either persuading or compelling his predecessor to pay up. Consequently plurality was encouraged and curates were put into many villages, where they could either rent a house of their own, live in lodgings or, like the celebrated Thomas Jones of Creaton in Northamptonshire, inhabit the local inn. This last was contrary to Canon Law; but homeless men cannot be choosey, and the Bishop of Peterborough, unable to provide Jones with anything better, conveniently turned a blind eye to his forty years' sojourn among the flesh pots and wine jars of Egypt! As late as 1835 William Cobbett estimated that there were 1,729 benefices without any parsonage house whatsoever; and 1,422 others where the house was unfit to live in. Furthermore, if parishes were counted in place of benefices, Cobbett added, then some 5,000 more parsonages were needed.

The over-large rectory at the beginning of the eighteenth century was now a rarity; but when it did exist it was usually in a sorry state. At Gotham in Nottinghamshire the Rector, William Bridges, complained in 1743: 'I have six score windows in the dwelling house, 8 staircases and not one good one; an hundred doors made out of sawn boards on ye premises.' However, as the century went on the agricultural revolution, and the greater prosperity of squire and parson, not only encouraged the former's younger son to take holy orders and occupy the family living, but also to improve the appearance, comfort, and amenities of the parsonage itself. This was the period when squires were remodelling their own homes on a more lordly scale; and sometimes the rectory was thrown in for good measure. The parsonage at Haughton, for instance, was entirely reconstructed about 1795 on a massive scale by the Yonges of Charnes Hall; while the O'Briens of Blatherwycke in Northamptonshire made imposing additions to their small seventeenth-century rectory. The parson himself, too, was becoming more society-conscious; his wife came from a better class in the community; and he was drawing higher tithes and glebe rents. This often added up to a new and grander home. John Leroo of Long Melford built himself a splendid new parsonage out of the wealth he amassed during the Napoleonic wars, which, when he had finished with it, contained sixteen rooms, besides the usual offices, a courtyard and a garden. The garden had taken the place of a former muddy farm-yard; and from now onwards it became the settled policy of the more genteel parson to push all evidence of his farming out of sight, if not out of mind. 'The farmyard must be cleared away entirely', declared Henry Crawford of his friend Edmund Bertram's new rectory at Thornton Lacey, 'and planted up to shut out the blacksmith's shop. The house must be turned to front the east, instead of the north; the entrance and principal rooms I mean must be on that side, where the view is really very pretty; I am sure it may be done. And there must be your approach through what is at present the garden. You must make a new garden, at what is now the back of the house; which will be giving it the best aspect in the world, sloping to the south east.'

Despite the advent of some parsons of Edmund Bertram's type, the utility house, the tumble-down house, and, indeed, the non-existent house continued to flourish in all too many parishes. Samuel Wesley's Rectory at Epworth was burnt down twice, once in 1702 and again in 1709. He rebuilt in solid and sensible fashion: 'a plain . . . complete old-fashioned family house', Dr Adam Clarke described it, 'and well suited for nineteen children. The attic floor is entirely from end-to-end of the whole building; the floor terraced and evidently designed for a repository of tithe corn, and where it could be kept cool and safe.' As far as the dilapidated vicarage is concerned there is no more pathetic cry from the heart than that of William Jones, curate of Broxbourne in Hertfordshire, which he confided to his diary on 24 August 1799: 'O that it was my lot to exchange this wretched, ruinous house for a comfortable cottage and a cheerful competence! How thankful to heaven I ought to be that the barn fell in the night-time. It might otherwise have been attended with the loss of many lives and the total ruin of my school.'

An Act of 1803 had ordered the clergy to reside in their parishes. Nevertheless during the first decade or two of the nineteenth century the abuses of absenteeism and plurality continued to flourish; while parsonage houses were still only too often conspicuous by their absence. The country clergy of this period were fond of inhabiting pleasant country towns like East Grinstead in Sussex or Louth in Lincolnshire, commonly known as 'the rookeries', whence in the summer months they might sally forth to do their Sunday duty. In winter-time it was a different story; for then they allowed their churches to stand closed and empty. Bishops Kaye and Jackson of Lincoln did their best to disturb such nests of rooks; but when the latter remonstrated with one absentee he was met with the retort: 'Satan himself, my lord, could not get there in the winter and I am always before him in the Spring.' Gradually matters improved, until most of the clergy became resident all the year round. That meant a house to live in; and since a higher percentage of the clergy than ever before were gentle-born men of means and culture, their new rectories or vicarages were as likely as not constructed on a lordly scale. Gone now were the long, low, thatched parsonages of the seventeenth and eighteenth centuries, with their rough farm buildings and muddy stable-yards. Instead drawing-room, dining-room, study, and morning-room took the place of the old hall with its parlours; while the kitchen quarters aped those of the big house in the park, with its servants' hall, butler's pantry, large kitchen, sculleries, and larder. These quarters were separated from the principal rooms by a green baise door and a long passageway.

At Foston-le-Clay in Yorkshire Sydney Smith built himself a comfortable and commodious house. He first employed an architect, who in 1813 produced some most elaborate and costly plans. 'You build for glory, sir; I for use', exclaimed Sydney, who thereupon became his own architect, carpenter, and mason. He even tried to make his own bricks from the clay of his glebe. 'I live trowel in hand', he wrote, 'my whole soul is filled up by lath and plaster.' When at last it was finished he remarked: 'I aimed at making it a snug parsonage and I think I have succeeded. . . . After finishing it I would not pay sixpence to alter it; but the expense of it will keep me a very poor man, a close prisoner here for my life, and render the education of my children a difficult exertion for me.' He spent in all some £4,000, part of which he borrowed from Queen Anne's Bounty. In 1829 Smith was appointed to Combe Florey near Taunton, where he found a charming but dilapidated rectory standing in its own woods. He rebuilt it at a cost of £2,000. Its principal feature was now the library, which was twenty-eight feet long and eight feet high, with a large bay window at one end. Its remaining walls were covered by books from floor to ceiling, all bound in vivid blues and reds.

In 1845 the advowson of the Rectory of Broughton in Lincolnshire was put up for sale, when the house was described as follows: 'A splendid and most complete brick-built and slated modern residence seated on a lawn, and approached by a carriage drive through shrubberies and plantations beautifully laid out. It contains on the first floor: four principal bedrooms, and five other chambers; on the ground floor: entrance hall and staircase, dining and drawing-rooms, and library, housekeeper's room, servants' hall, two kitchens, pantry and larder, wine and beer cellars in the basement. An extensive walled-in garden, large greenhouse with vinery, paved yard, a brick-built and slated 3-stall stable with lofts over, harness-house, double coach-house, brewhouse and bakehouse; knife coal and wash-houses. In the farmyard: brick-built and tiled stables, granary, cowhouse and piggeries. Ninety-four acres of glebe-land.'

The history of High Wych Vicarage in Hertfordshire was a good example of the kind of parsonage now being erected. The rough and lonely hamlet of High Wych was originally part of the Vicarage of Sawbridgeworth; but in the eighteen-sixties it was made into a separate parish to satisfy the needs of a squarson named Frank Johnson, who some twenty years later became Bishop of Colchester. Johnson built the church, school, curatage, a number of cottages, and his own vicarage, very largely out of his own pocket. The vicarage was on a most lavish scale with some sixteen principal rooms; a garden complete with hot-houses, walled kitchen garden, orchards, broad lawns, a terrace for peacocks, and a small swimming pool; and the whole place was surrounded by many acres of meadowland, through which a long gravel drive ran to iron gates, guarded by a lodge. The population of the entire parish was only a few hundreds.

When Robert Hawker was instituted to Morwenstow in 1834, the Bishop told him: 'You will have to build a house on the glebe, Mr H.' Hawker, like Sydney Smith, was his own architect; and both men incorporated queer whimsies of their own devising. Smith kept his fires bright by cunningly contrived air-tubes; while Hawker constructed his chimneys to represent models of the church towers he had known. 'The kitchen chimney', he wrote to a friend, 'perplexed me very much, till I bethought me of my mother's tomb; and there it is, in its exact shape and dimensions.'

A number of Victorian parsonages were adaptations of or additions to older seventeenth- or eighteenth-century houses. The Rectory of Creeton in Lincolnshire is a fine illustration of one such evolution. The original structure of a central hall, flanked by a kitchen on one side and a parlour on the other, with three bedrooms above, was gradually extended. First in 1824 the kitchen quarters were enlarged; then, during the eighteen-fifties a suitably imposing frontage was added; and finally in 1880 an annex of red-brick was built onto an otherwise stone house. Occasionally one has the curious experience of finding the actual original houses of this evolution still existing independently in the same parish. At Warmington there is a sixteenth-century vicarage known as the 'Glebe-house', that undoubtedly incorporates part of an older medieval building; a late seventeenth- or early eighteenth-century vicarage near the church, which is miscalled today 'the Old Rectory', since Warmington Rectory was appropriated in the thirteenth century; and finally the present substantial Victorian house that was erected in 1885.

The Victorian golden age bred the squarson, who sometimes occupied the manor house itself and fully lived up to its traditions. An outstanding instance was that of Sabine Baring-Gould, who inherited the living and manor house of Lew Trenchard in Devon. When he arrived in 1881 he found 'a flat-surfaced stucco building, two storied, the front broken by a commonplace glass porch'. But as a boy of sixteen Baring-Gould had made a resolve that if ever the house became his he would extend and beautify it; and now he set to work. He, too, was his own architect, but a skilful and indefatigable one; and by his death in 1924 Lew House had become an imposing mansion.

At Great Doddington near Wellingborough, the Vicar, Maiz Gregory, who was also the Marquis of Northampton's agent, persuaded the latter to restore the old manor house at a cost of nearly £500, and to let it to him as a vicarage in 1869. His successors continued to live there; and eventually the house was bought by the Church Commissioners in 1922. It is still the vicarage today; and recently another £500 were spent on repairs. Other earlier examples of ancient manor houses, that are still parsonages, can be seen at Great Ponton and Corby Glen in Lincolnshire. The former is an early Tudor house scheduled as an ancient monument; while the latter is a seventeenth-century building of Cotswold style, that first became the vicarage in the eighteenth century.

The Victorian parsonage was not merely imposing in its structure and ample proportions; but was often splendidly furnished and equipped with all the latest devices. *The Standard Magazine* wrote of Morwenstow Vicarage on 1 September 1875: 'Within the rooms are full of quaint old oak, curious china, and antiquities of all sorts, much of it gathered in the parish at a time when such things were less sought after than at present. . . . There are one or two fine old bedsteads; and we remember Mr Hawker tell with much effect the many devices which he had to practice before getting the finest of them into his possession. He was unsuccessful until he represented to the owner the number of persons who must have died in that bed, and this frightened him into sparing it.' Sydney Smith, on the other hand, believed in furnishing his home to suit his needs. 'Every room', we are told, 'had the furniture and fittings exactly suited to its requirements; simplicity was the keynote, convenience the object.'

There is little doubt that during this period of unexampled peace and prosperity so-called improvements went on being added to many parsonages, almost as a matter of course, right down to the 1914-18 War, when they ended abruptly. The pattern of such improvements is familiar enough: increasing the size of already over-large rooms, putting in new windows, multiplying the number of bedrooms, adding verandas and conservatories, and filling the gardens with rustic summerhouses, fountains, sundials, and statuary. Joseph Holmes, who was Vicar of Swineshead in Lincolnshire from 1848 to 1911, is reliably reported to have made a new bay window in his vicarage after the birth of each of his numerous daughters; while Henry Lipscomb, Vicar of Sawbridgeworth, added extensively to his house after the birth of his fifth child in 1882.

No doubt much of this new building was necessary. Country

parsons possessed big families, frequently kept pupils, and employed a large staff of servants. Not all the clergy, however, could afford to pay for their homes out of their own pockets; but found a generous patron in the Church Commissioners or Queen Anne's Bounty Office. In order to encourage a resident ministry, particularly in the new housing areas, the Commissioners obtained statutory authority for spending a million pounds of their capital on new parsonage houses; and when in 1875 this sum was exhausted they got similar permission for using another million. Q.A.B., too, were very ready to make loans or even grants for similar purposes. Francis Goddard, who was presented to the Vicarage of Hilmarton in Wiltshire in 1858, later wrote in his *Reminiscences*: 'The house was extremely well built, and the original building has never had a crack or settlement in it: the cost of it was raised by a loan from Queen Anne's Bounty Office, for a period of 30 or 32 years, the interest and a portion of capital to be paid yearly, charged upon the annual proceeds of the Vicarage. The sum borrowed was £960 and to liquidate the whole and receive back the cancelled bond I paid in capital and interest about £700. I also spent in additions to the house (for there were few offices in the original building) in offices and outbuildings and other additions about £400 when I entered upon the living, and there were a good many alterations made in the interior of the house.' At Creeton a loan of £450 for thirty years was made to enable the Rector to enlarge his parsonage for a school, although the population of the village was only eighty. When the old Vicarage at Takeley in Essex practically collapsed in 1875, a new and imposing brick house was erected the following year and paid for by the Church Commissioners.

The practice of adding to and increasing the amenities of the parsonage went merrily on until the Great War. But from 1918 onwards it was a very different story, in face of constantly rising prices and wages, and the difficulty of obtaining domestic servants. Furthermore, as the older incumbents died or retired it became increasingly difficult to compel their heirs to meet the dilapidations bill in full, since they had not the means to pay. Consequently the Church began in certain cases to adopt the expedient of selling the old large rectory and grounds, and building a new and much smaller one on glebe land out of the proceeds. At High Wych, for example, after the death in 1928 of the Revd Horace Rackham, who had been incumbent there for forty-one years, his dilapidations were assessed at over £1,000. Rather than enforce them the old Vicarage was sold for a mere £2,000, and in 1932 a snug, solid, not unpleasing little house, with a small garden, was erected on one corner of the glebe meadows.

Sometimes, alas, this policy was pursued over-enthusiastically and did not always meet with the success anticipated. Many fine houses, in fact, were thrown haphazard onto the market and sold for a song, with little or no regard to the ultimate interests of the parishes they served. The President of Jesus College wrote recently: 'In the early thirties a good Vicarage near Cambridge was sold for something over £500 to serve as a Boys' Home.' At King's Cliffe in Northamptonshire during the late 'twenties a fine rectory set in beautiful grounds and in a reasonable state of repair, realized only £300 for demolition. But, perhaps, most scandalous of all the splendid rectory of Asheldam in Essex, with its forty acres of glebe, made a miserable £800. It is of interest to see what happened to these particular houses. The Cambridge vicarage is now worth 'three or four thousand pounds'. Part of the King's Cliffe Rectory was converted into a bungalow and made several thousand pounds profit for the wise builder who had invested in it. Finally Asheldam Rectory and its glebe became a fruit farm and fetched £25,000. To this one could add that the Cambridge vicarage 'is to be separated from the neighbouring parish to which it had been united, and it will be necessary . . . to provide a house for the parson'; while King's Cliffe has also recently been re-created an independent benefice, and a Rectory purchased at the cost of £2,350.

Modern parsonages, where they are built, usually run to double or treble the sum for which the old ones were sold; and their cramped quarters, tiny gardens, and general meanness of design represent a striking and melancholy commentary on the declining position of the parson in the countryside. Some are nothing more or less than council houses, naked and unashamed. Thousands of pounds, too, are required to recondition old parsonages. An estimate drawn up in 1957 to reconstruct the existing rectory of Bulwick in Northamptonshire ran to as much as £5,000. And yet, when the work is completed, they still remain old buildings, and a heavy yearly dilapidation charge is immediately clapped upon them.

The evolution of the parsonage successfully mirrored in every age the place and importance of the incumbent in village life. The tiny medieval shanty, situated in or near the churchyard, bespoke the simple peasant priest ever ready by his church to meet the spiritual needs of his people; while the rough, outlying farm buildings proclaimed his close connection with the soil and his obligation, like his rustic parishioners, to win his living by the sweat of his brow and the labour of his hands. The more comfortable and commodious farmhouse parsonages of Elizabethan and early Stuart England denoted the growing material prosperity of at least some of the country clergy; and the aping of the manor house by the few foreshadowed the successful social climber. The dearth of country parsonages throughout the eighteenth and early nineteenth centuries was no doubt partly due to the destruction of the Civil Wars, from which they were slow to recover; but also to the rapid growth of absenteeism and plurality during that period. But as the eighteenth century drew to its close some rectories and vicarages were rebuilt or remodelled as the gentleman-country-parson began to make his appearance. These last were much more comfortable and elegant than their predecessors; for the parson's wife was no longer being drawn exclusively from farm, rectory, or the domestic staff of a big house. It was sometimes becoming the fashion for the squire to marry off an unattractive daughter to the curate, who might then be presented to the family living. Professional men, too, whether in Medicine, the Law or the Civil Service, began to contract alliances with the clergy.

The sixteenth- or seventeenth-century parson's wife had mainly busied herself with her family and domestic concerns; and took little part in the work of the parish, beyond encouraging her husband in the conscientious discharge of his duties. Mrs John Wade, the wife of the curate-in-charge of Hammersmith after the Restoration, for instance, told him: 'When you have been at prayer with any of your parish never grudge or think much at it if you find your body a little spent or tired. Say "So long as my body is not wasted in a way of sin I am cheerful and contented; so long as I can spend myself in the work of God and service of souls I am not troubled at all at it but satisfied in it".' Her better-class eighteenth-century successor might occasionally visit the sick or relieve the needy; but the spectacle of a Susannah Wesley or Mary Fletcher teaching their parishioners was a startling and unpalatable one. It was left to the Victorian parsonage to turn parochial chores into a family concern. The wife played the organ, presided over the Mothers' Meeting, visited the sick and old, organized the Missionary bazaar in the rectory garden; and was, indeed, always on the go, hastening from one end of the village to the other on foot or in her pony cart intent on good works. Her daughters taught in the Sunday School and assisted their mother until such time as they married curates and set up for themselves. The sons were not so easily harnessed to the parish pump. At the universities they acquired the reputation of being gay young dogs, who, having broken away from the sanctity of the Establishment, were determined to make the most of sowing their wild oats. But in the vacations it was often a different story. Then they would sedately read the lessons at Mattins and Evensong, give a series of lectures in the school, and organize church or missionary plays.

Old Takeley Vicarage, which collapsed in 1875.

New Takeley Vicarage, built in 1876–7.

High Wych Vicarage, built in 1863; the Revd. H. F. Rackham with his wife and friends

The Revd. Robert Hart and his daughter; Greenstead Green Vicarage, Essex, about 1900.

The parsonage, in fact, had now firmly established itself as the hub of village life round which everything else revolved; a state of affairs that reached its peak in the late Victorian and Edwardian era. To the rectory field the children went for their summer Sunday School treat, where they consumed mountains of sticky buns and slab cake; after which they ran races and sang songs. In the New Year they met again in the rectory barn for tea and a Christmas tree. 'We invited all the children day or Sunday School', Richard Seymour of Kinwarton recorded in his diary on 1 January 1854, 'and their mothers, and 2 or 3 others with children. All mothers and children were well and not inconveniently packed into the room. The invitation was for 4 oclock, and at 4.30 we began with a song of praise . . . then tea. 16 loaves (but small on account of the prices) were all eaten. The cake was abundant. We sang twice more in the course of the tea. . . . After tea others came in, and I think we must have numbered 190. At about 5.30 pm we lighted up the Tree, putting out the lights. Sang (after a few words from me) Neale's Christmas hymn, and then I distributed prints to the 20 best in conduct and attendance. Then cut off and distributed the fruit of the Tree, singing at intervals, ending with God save the Queen.'

The rectory had always been given to hospitality. Chaucer's 'poore parson' we can be sure was pleased to welcome his neighbours into his humble home, since:

> To cursen for his tithes ful lothe was he,
> But rather wolde he given out of doute,
> Unto his pore parishioners aboute.

George Herbert's 'Country Parson' certainly invited his parishioners into his home: 'So that in the compass of the year, he hathe them all with him, because country people are very observant of such things, and will not be persuaded, but not being invited, they are hated.' These people he would have entertained in his hall or principal room; where, too, at a later date the tithe dinner or 'frolic' might also be held. The annual tithe dinner, an occasion for much hard drinking and merrymaking, grew up with the substitution of cash for kind in the payment of tithes and rents. Parson Woodeforde has recorded many such repasts in his diary, with a minute account of the vast quantities of food and beer consumed. This 'jam' concealed the unpleasing 'powder' of having to pay up afterwards:

> At length the busy time begins,
> 'come neighbours, we must wag . . . '
> The money chinks, down drop their chins,
> Each lugging out his bag.

K

My grandfather, Robert Hart, who was Vicar of Takeley from 1868 to 1896, used to say that the big farmers sent cheques, but the small tithe payers, who owed him only a few pounds, turned up regularly in order to consume what they could of it in cold beef and beer. The collection of the tithe by Queen Anne's Bounty Office finally put an end to this festive gathering; although by that time most parsons themselves had dropped it, preferring to employ a lawyer to recover their tithes for them. At Hitcham J. S. Henslow had aroused the wrath of the farmers by suppressing his audit dinner as early as the eighteen-forties, since it had become an excuse for much intemperance; and used the money instead for a village recreation fund. In Victorian times the rectory garden party made its appearance. There were sometimes three of them: for the villagers, for the farmers, and for the neighbouring clergy and gentry. Croquet parties became the vogue, derived from the game of pall-mall; a gentle, leisurely pastime, terminated by a lavish supper. Ladies in crinolines, ready-made for this occasion, concealed the ball, which was then stealthily kicked into an advantageous position.

Above all, by the late nineteenth century, the parsonage had developed into a centre of culture and learning, that set the moral and educational as well as the spiritual standards of the village. The seventeenth-century clergy had possibly catechized the village children in their 'hall'; and Laurence Sterne, author of *Tristram Shandy* and Vicar of Sutton-on-the-Forrest in Yorkshire, used regularly during Lent, as he informed the Archbishop in 1743, 'to explain our religion to the children and servants of my parishioners in my own house every Sunday night . . . from six oclock until nine.' Confirmation classes, as held today, were unknown in the eighteenth century; and even as late as 1840 Francis Goddard, then curate of Winterbourne Bassett, expressed surprise at finding a confirmation class for girls in progress in the drawing-room at Broad Hinton Vicarage presided over by the Revd E. W. Tufnell. But with the advent of the Oxford Movement this type of class at the parsonage quickly established itself. Well-to-do rectors were not averse from turning their large homes into coaching establishments for the Universities, Army or Civil Service examinations. A. G. Bradley in *Exmoor Memories*, as we have already heard, narrated how he, as one of a succession of dull or backward public school boys, was thus instructed in the 'sixties by the old Oxford blue and sporting parson, Robert Martin of Challacombe in north Devon; and was also taught how to handle a rod and gun. The arrival of these pupils often meant the enlargement of the parsonage. At Hatfield Broad Oak, for instance, Francis Galpin, an authority on musical instruments, was obliged to increase the size of his

vicarage in order to accommodate his scholars. And Edward
Sylvester, the wealthy Rector of Deene in Northamptonshire from
1873 to 1895, actually built on a new wing to an already big house
for a choir school. The latter, I am reliably informed, employed a
staff of at least fifteen servants.

So in every aspect of life the nineteenth-century rectory had
become an oasis of cultured and gracious living in the midst of what
was still only too often a savage or boorish village community,
shedding its beneficent rays far and wide. Unhappy was the parish
that, for one reason or another, did not possess one. Robert Hawker
wrote over the porch of his own vicarage at Morwenstow;

> A house, a glebe, a pound a day,
> A pleasant place to watch and pray:
> Be true to Church, be kind to poor,
> O minister for evermore!

But we must not run away with the idea that in this golden Victorian age all parsonages were as comfortable or as pleasant as a
nostalgia for the 'Good Old Days' sometimes makes us imagine.
There were always plenty of poor parsons and parsonages about,
where life was rough and hard. Generally speaking it would be true
to say that the richer houses were to be found in the south and east
of the country, particularly near London and in the wealthier
agricultural districts; while the smaller, poorer, and ruder dwellings
would be located in the north and west. There were, we know,
fortress parsonages on the Scottish border, like Embleton; and in
the Lake District Wordsworth described a typical rectory in the
*Excursion* when he wrote:

> All unembowered
> And naked stood that lowly parsonage.

On the windswept heights of Trentislow in north Devon during the
late 'sixties stood a vicarage, where, wrote a contemporary, there
'were boarded floors and the plainest of furniture and all the signs of
narrow means . . . the Vicar, an able scholar, was educating all his
boys, and possibly his girls too, in this little storm-beaten vicarage.
. . . There were no guns or rods or horses up there to relieve the
dreariness.'

Today the modern parsonage appears to be fast losing its grip on
its more sophisticated and much better-off parishioners. Small in
size, with a minute garden, it has not the facilities for catering for
large numbers or mass meetings. The village garden fête committee
looks round for another site; the secular village hall, run independently of the Church, supplies most of the recreational needs of the

parish; the county school, with its up-to-date headmaster and young keen teachers fresh from their training colleges, becomes the centre of learning and culture; and above all the welfare state now provides the loaves and fishes, once so readily forthcoming from the rectory kitchen. In any case the parson's wife is no longer there to look after these things. She has gone out to work in order to pay for the education of her children; a task that can no longer be adequately undertaken by the Rector in his study. *Sic gloria mundi passit.*

## CHAPTER IX

# The Present Position 1958

IN THE PAST the Rector was an employer on a fairly extensive scale; and he also acted as an unofficial poor-relief officer to his necessitous flock. His wife was often the lady bountiful of the village, who could always be relied upon to provide bowls of soup, old clothes, and nourishing invalid foods almost at a moment's notice. Furthermore the Victorian parson could rely automatically on certain mechanics of his ministry. The church, for example, whatever his parishioners' personal opinion concerning himself, would always be reasonably full. The children, without the need for bribing or goading, could be relied upon to come regularly to Sunday School, where there were plenty of young teachers ready and able to instruct them. The repair of the church itself, even after the Church Rate had been abolished, was scarcely a burden, since the squire, farmers, and indeed the Rector himself were cheerfully prepared to shoulder the bulk of the expense, without the need for wearisome appeals to the parish. Parochial financial troubles as such, in fact, hardly existed. Village entertainments like concerts, penny-readings, lectures, teas, and suppers, were arranged solely for the benefit and amusement of the inhabitants, not in order to empty their pockets. Their 'Betters' provided the money required for such laudable objects as foreign missions or school parties and prizes; while the diocese as yet made few or no demands on its country parishes. There was plenty of cheap or 'voluntary' labour for parish chores. Consequently the Rector was enabled to do his proper work in cushioned ease. There was no need for him to perform household tasks or labour in his garden; he did not have to pull his own church bell or stoke its furnace or act the part of clerk and verger. The singing he could safely leave to the choir and the Sunday School to its band of faithful teachers. There was no scarcity of women cleaners to keep the interior of the church spotless or of willing helpers to assist at parochial functions. The parson could, therefore, safely get on with his job of teaching and studying, visiting and worshipping, without having to concern himself unduly over the 'serving of tables'.

The picture is a very different one in the nineteen-fifties. In the first place the average country parson is now a comparatively poor man. He can afford little in charity; and employs no-one in his house or garden beyond the occasional char-woman or casual labourer. He himself must often go cap-in-hand to his parochial church council and ask them to help towards the payment of his rates and dilapidations; and he looks to the diocese to bring the endowed income of his living up to a minimum standard. These minimum stipends vary in different areas; but by and large they hover round the £600 mark—scarcely a lordly income for a professional man, whose specialized qualifications are usually of a very high order. However, by means of a variety of ingenious devices he is enabled to keep up a reasonably prosperous appearance: dressing well, running a new car, and sending his children to good schools. This is achieved at the expense of his proper clerical functions. He was ordained to serve a *cura animarum*; instead he spends much of his time clerking, teaching, examining, or taking services in neighbouring parishes during sequestrations, of which nowadays there are an inordinate number, simply for his own personal profit. His wife probably goes out to work; and if he also happens to inhabit a large rectory or vicarage, he can make a considerable income by letting rooms. This is all wrong. If the country parson is still needed in the village and there is enough work for him to do there, he should be paid a salary by the Church commensurate with his abilities and qualifications; and not be burdened with the extra worry and wear-and-tear of having to find the additional means for making both ends meet.

For the Rector today, unlike his Victorian predecessors, quickly discovers that in a small rural parish he has to do practically everything himself. Dr Geoffrey Soden, writing of his experiences as Rector of Shipmeadow and Barsham in Suffolk from 1944 to 1956, declared: 'In a small country village the priest has to be his own sacristan, he looks after the linen, changes the frontals, lights the sanctuary lamp, sees the cassocks are repaired, rings the bell on week-days and Sundays, hoes the church paths, trims the hedges and even scythes the churchyard. The parson, too, may have to grow the flowers for the church, besides arranging and looking after them during the week. He will undoubtedly have to raise hundreds of pounds for the restoration of the fabric of both his churches.' Every evening a country incumbent used to walk down to the local level crossing to watch the express go through. When a friend asked him why he did so, he replied, 'Well, I have to run everything in this parish. I have to collect stuff for the Jumble Sale; I have to see that the Youth Club doesn't collapse when the members quarrel. I arrange the parish outings and, of course, manage the church and school accounts. So I enjoy coming down to look at the one thing in the parish that I don't run.'

The upkeep of large medieval churches in tiny village communities that have lost their squires and are probably served by non-resident incumbents, is one of the problems that the Church as a whole is finding extremely difficult to solve. It is true that the inhabitants of any particular village, whether church-goers or not, will respond nobly to a call for funds to save their parish church. But, alas, it is now no longer a question of raising a few hundred pounds; for the estimates run into thousands. Outside help is not always easy to obtain; and, indeed, unless many of these churches are to be allowed slowly to deteriorate and collapse into ruins, the only ultimate solution appears to be to hand them over to the Ministry of Works. A policy of patch-and-mend and hope-for-the-best cannot be maintained indefinitely. The operation of the Church's new Inspection Measure, is bound, as soon as it gets fully under way, to disclose an appalling and overwhelming mass of decay that is quite incapable of being met by voluntary contributions.

Then it can be argued that the modern parson's wife, the unpaid curate on whose shoulders in the past so much of the work of a parish lay, is, in an ever-growing number of villages, no longer playing her part on the old scale. The bachelor incumbent is far less of a rarity than he used to be; while many of the wives of the clergy now go out to work or busy themselves exclusively with the running of their own homes. The disappearance of 'nanny' and the domestic servant, together with straitened financial circumstances, largely account for her waning parochial influence. But there is more to it than that. Some clergy deliberatly discourage their ladies from taking an active part in parish work. As one incumbent said to me recently: 'I stand between my wife and the parish.'

Since the end of the second world war village life has been changing rapidly. In place of the pre-1914 'yokel', who could barely read or write, rarely left the village, regularly attended his parish church, and accepted unquestioningly the essential rightness of the Victorian social order, a generation has grown up in the countryside with an entrirely different outlook. With money to burn, small families to maintain, and a taste for pleasure and excitement, the modern villager is continually on the move. There is an insatiable urge to get away from the village into the nearest town for shopping and the cinema; and further afield in the summer months by bus, car, or motor-bicycle. Holidays are long and elaborate; television aerials appear in ever increasing numbers; toys for the children get bigger and better; clothes are fashionable and expensive; and much money is expended on luxuries that their parents would never have dreamed of. The overall effect is to make the younger generation less village-conscious, and far less church-conscious than their forbears. It is becoming very much of an uphill battle to attract the young people to the official church services, which they regard as dull and boring, or to maintain the old-fashioned Sunday School or youth organiza-tion. The days, too, when Heaven and Hell loomed large in the villagers' minds are gone. They expect to be bribed; and in this respect the welfare state has much more to offer than the Church-in-the-Country.

Country parsons in some of the tinier and more remote villages and hamlets are faced, indeed, with their gradual dissolution. The big house has probably been pulled down or sold for an institution; the school has been closed and the children are transported by bus every morning to some larger centre of population; while the young married couples move away into the nearest town, where council houses are being erected. The local authorities will not build houses in hamlets where there is no deep drainage. The steady drift from the land, which is accentuated by the mechanization of agriculture, is also helping to empty the villages; and the discomforts of the old-fashioned 'tied' cottages do not encourage families to dig in their roots. These last, in fact, all too often accommodate mere 'birds of passage', who never develop any communal consciousness at all. The bigger village, conveniently situated on a main road, within easy reach of a town, and boasting its own council houses and light industries, is, of course, in a very different position. Here, from the parson's point of view, the danger lies more in secularization than disintegration. The focal points of such parishes are too often the undenominational village hall and the county school rather than the church.

The country clergy themselves are not only vividly aware of these facts and problems; but their own lives are affected by them. In the first place they have become more mobile than ever before. Despite his knowledge that the average country benefice now provides a minimum income that is much the same wherever he goes, while the expenses and inconveniences of removals are considerable, an incumbent rarely stays more than from five to seven years in any one parish. He has no intention, like his nineteenth-century pre-decessor, of settling down for life and digging in his roots. Why is he so restless? No doubt he has become infected by the rootless, rest-less atmosphere of his time. He sees others on the move and feels bound to follow them. He no longer has the patience for the long, slow haul, but seeks for quick, spectacular results before his popularity has begun to wane; and he quickly tires of the same faces and the old routine. He constantly deplores what he calls 'getting

into a rut'. 'Let it not be said of the parson', wrote Mrs Kathleen
Jarvis in her amusing *Impressions of a Parson's Wife*, 'that he allows
himself to become, through long residence upon one living, a kind
of holy vegetable.' Our present Theological Colleges probably con-
centrate too much upon training ordinands for the towns. In the
past a man went up to the university from his native village and
returned to it, or to one close by, after ordination; and proceeded to
make that place the scene of his life's work. Today the young
deacon is sent into a town, where he stays for some years. Later,
when he finds himself in the country, his techniques of worship and
pastoralia prove inadequate; but instead of sitting down to learn his
new job among people who value a good cricketer or a knowledgeable gardener better than a fine preacher or musician, he grows dis-
heartened and moves on elsewhere, ever seeking for the ideal parish
that will appreciate him at his own valuation.

Secondly, the modern country parson usually finds that he is
called upon to administer two, three, or even more rural parishes.
For the old twin evils of plurality and non-residence have been
revived on a large scale, with this difference: that whereas in the past
the non-resident incumbent normally installed a curate of sorts in
his place, today our Diocesan Authorities, relying upon the motor
car, expect one man to run single-handed a number of separate
parishes. Technically, indeed, these parishes are 'united'; but in
practice each of them continues to operate as an independent unit,
with its own church services, churchwardens, parochial church
council, Mothers' Union, and separate financial accounts. Neither
will such 'united' parishes co-operate to any great extent. Each one
expects the incumbent to spend the bulk of his time in their village,
and resents the demands of the rest. No-one likes these unions, least
of all the parson himself. They have been brought about because of
the pressure of inflation, a shortage of ordination candidates, and the
dwindling populations of many small villages and hamlets. The
Revd C. L. S. Linnell, Rector of three Norfolk livings, wrote in
1956: 'Woe betide the pluralist incumbent of today who thinks he
can pool things! Country people are tenacious of their rights and
loyalties to their particular parish church. . . . They expect to
work separately and the incumbent in my position must expect to
have three sets of churchwardens, three parochial church councils,
three organists, three of everything.'

This type of plurality, with its exhausting demands on the physical and spiritual powers of the priest, may well partly account for
his brief tenure of any particular grouping. Some of these groupings
have swollen to an inordinate size and largely defeat their own purposes. For example the Isham experiment in the Peterborough

diocese, where six parishes were grouped under a rector and two curates, broke down because the curates, when they left, could not be replaced. The largest plurality at present in existence is probably the Lincolnshire grouping that contains ten originally independent benefices: Ormsby, Ketsby, Calceby, Driby, Harrington, Brinkhill, Somersby, Bag-Enderby, Tetford, and Salmonby. Another smaller pooling in the same diocese consists of five parishes: Rapsley, Somerby, Great Humby, Little Humby, Saperton, and Braceby. Others could easily be cited; and, indeed, the whole trend of diocesan thinking is towards their multiplication. It is most unusual for a parish, which has once been united with others, to regain its independence.

The whole question of the parson's freehold is today very much in the melting pot. In the past this freehold has provided the country clergy with an independence that has bred a type of parson who has been of great value to the community. The country priest often has to face poverty, loneliness, misunderstanding, and difficulties of every kind in his pastoral work. His independence was sometimes the only firm ground he had under his feet. Parishioners could bluster, the Bishop might prove unsympathetic; but the parson could not be bullied or unseated. On the other hand this privilege has sometimes been abused by misfits; and the question is being more and more insistently asked, particularly by the laity: why, when even fellowships at the ancient universities are no longer being held for life, should the clergy alone retain the corporation sole? A number of Clergy Discipline Measures have, of course, shorn the freehold of its pristine glory; but even so it is still extremely difficult to get rid of an unpopular or lazy incumbent. 'The humblest Rector or Vicar', wrote the Revd D. L. Scott, Rector of Rippingale in Lincolnshire, voicing the parson's point of view, 'however small and remote his cure, enjoys a freedom and responsibility such as survive in few other walks of life in this bureaucratic age. These surely are not unworthy things to be aspired after, and they go a long way towards out-weighing whatever disadvantage may accompany them.' But, despite a stubborn rear-guard action, it appears likely that the abolition of the freehold is only a matter of time. In that case the power of the Bishop over his clergy would be vastly increased, and the work of the Church would no doubt correspondingly benefit. But with the advent of such regimentation the traditional country parson, as he has figured in these pages, would become extinct.

So much for the present position of the country parson. It is neither a happy nor a secure one, and tends to induce at once a sense of failure and apprehension. It is scarcely an encouragement to

others to follow in his footsteps. But there is another side to the
picture. It can be convincingly argued that the Church of England
has and always must look to the little country parish for the living
waters of her spiritual strength. In the great industrial centres the
religious life of the people is disintegrating in a feverish round of
activities that lead nowhere; while the clergy themselves are
becoming more and more obsessed with their 'visible' congregations at the expense of the mass of their largely 'invisible' parishioners. In the villages, on the other hand, a balance and harmony
between parson and people, priest and laity, the past and the present,
the sanctified grace of the Church and the natural grace of the
peasant, can often still be found. In a country rectory there is still
sufficient leisure and peace available for quiet prayer, study, and
contemplation; for the growth and development of a healthy family
life, based on the Book of Common Prayer and the natural cycle of
the country seasons; and for the exercise of a ministry that is truly
pastoral and not party. 'The life of the rural priesthood', wrote the
Revd J. H. Jacques, another country parson, 'is a mixed life, at once
active and contemplative. It is a life of prayer and worship, a life of
visiting and service, a life of thought and study, and a life lived in
close contact with the things of the spirit. His is the task of turning a
natural community into an international one by his prayers, his
leading in worship, and his spiritual teaching.'

The village community normally respects the parson, loves its
ancient church, in whose churchyard its ancestors lie buried, and
jealously treasures its past history. When the need arises it will make
every effort to preserve and repair the church, retain its parson, and
safeguard its own independence. The incumbent himself, once he
has been accepted by the village, can do pretty much what he likes
in the way of ceremonial or the absence of it, in holding many
services or few. Villagers, however, will resent a continual demand
for money; and the parson who is no more than a mere money-raiser,
will never be truly liked. The priest they want, and indeed have
always wanted, is the man who will love them and help them, meet
them in their own homes as well as in the church or village hall,
interest himself in their children, and cheerfully shoulder the uncon-
genial job that no-one else will do. Such a parson, declared Mr
Jacques, 'has to learn the hard way that the only thing that matters
is charity; a charity in which he hopes his people will receive him
with all his failings, while he accepts them with all their sins.'

Is there any future for the country parson? In his recent book,
*Sparrows of the Spirit*, F. H. West concluded his story of the village
clergyman since the Reformation as follows: 'The future is uncertain, but one thing is sure: even if the great cities were to lie

desolate and the plane were banished from the sky, there must always be seedtime and harvest. The country parson with the dust of the field in his shoes ministers now where man must labour till man has ceased to walk the face of the earth.' E. W. Martin wrote in *The Secret People* on a less optimistic note: 'Religion in many country parishes has become a dreary affair—few people attend church or chapel, and those who do are rarely prepared to accept the ethical standards of their faith as a basis for living.' Village regeneration, he believed, no longer depended upon the spiritual leadership of the parson, who in all too many cases might be classed with the sickle or the horse plough, 'as something the country people have outgrown.' His place in rural life is being largely taken over by the owner-occupier farmer.

Another, anonymous, modern writer in a savage onslaught on the country priest was even more brutally frank: 'Many signs proclaim that the existence of the country parson, as he has developed since the Reformation, is doomed. The countryside no longer needs him, and is largely indifferent to his passing.'[1]

It must, of course, be admitted that the country clergy today have neither the influence nor the following in the countryside that they once possessed. The system of plurality and union is bound to be unpopular; and where the parson himself is non-resident church membership and enthusiasm sometimes decline at an alarming rate. Then the clergy themselves are in short supply. Every three parishes out of four in England are rural, yet less than one out of every five persons lives in the country. And since money is also scarce, the Church's planners are encouraged to cut down the clerical labour force in rural areas. We live in a statistical age, there is magic in numbers, and it is sometimes felt that each parson should be allocated so many thousand 'patients' apiece like his counterpart in general medical practice. Regular church attenders in the village may, on the average, be more numerous than in the towns; but nevertheless it is distinctly discouraging for the Rector over the years to muster a congregation of no more than twenty or thirty regular worshippers out of a total population of three or four hundred souls. The policy of amalgamation may in some ways be that of despair, but it is also certainly one of convenience and relative efficiency. As such it is likely to be increasingly pursued in the future.

One result of the inflationary spiral on the Church of England has been to reduce her clergy to a dependence and servility such as they have never known before. 'By a quiet revolution', wrote the Archdeacon of Lincoln to *The Times* in the summer of 1957, 'the

[1] See, *The Modern Churchman*, Vol. XIII, No.4, December 1952. 'As We Are In The Country Church' by 'Countryman'.

*'Don't worry, old fellow, the decision is mine.'*

parochial clergy of the Church of England are being transformed into the salaried members of a diocesan staff, living in houses provided and maintained for them, on incomes fixed and guaranteed by a diocesan fund.' The village parson of yesterday asked little from and owed even less to his diocese. He lived off his glebe, tithes, fees, and perquisites, all of which were found within his parish; while his freehold gave him complete freedom of action within its boundaries. Legally the parsonage house was the property of the sitting incumbent, and he was solely responsible for its repair and upkeep. Now the pattern has completely changed. The majority of country parsons depend for the bulk of their income upon diocesan grants; and the diocese provides the money for dilapidations and rates that the clergy are unable to screw out of their parochial church councils. Inevitably, then, the parson loses some of his independence. The diocese pays the piper; and therefore not unnaturally expects to be allowed to plan for the parishes, using the clergy more and more as its willing instruments for raising the necessary funds in their villages and implementing to the best of their ability the resolutions passed at the Diocesan Conference; resolutions drawn up at the centre, but which rarely meet with any serious opposition from either clergy or laity on the floor of the Conference.

The social change in the clergy themselves is also worthy of remark. The village parson is no longer automatically associated with the manorial class. The Oxford or Cambridge M.A. hood is not so frequently to be seen as of yore in our country churches; and the priest and his wife are not quite so obviously a gentleman and lady. In fact it is quite probable that an elderly rural rector today is not, as one might well suppose, coming to the end of a longish ministry, but has been recently ordained, after retiring from another profession or occupation; and has never attended a university at all. 'The country church today,' declared Dr H. E. Bracey, 'includes men who have been commercial travellers, civil servants, soldiers, sailors, schoolteachers, farmers, engineers, and business men.' Most of these have been under discipline of one kind or another for the greater part of their lives, and consequently are not so touchy as the old-time parson in the matter of their independence and freehold.

Nevertheless despite all these adverse factors and apparent handicaps there is no reason to expect any early or final extinction of the country parson. No doubt his critics would like to see him swept away into the limbo that has already received his former ally and lay-opposite, the squire; but his should prove a far tougher and more adaptable personality. There can be no return, of course, to the golden age or to his ancient glories; but provided the Church is not quite so foolish as to abandon the parochial system in the countryside altogether, a place may yet be found for him in these new, exciting, revolutionary times in which we live.

What are the methods best calculated to achieve this end? In order to prevent present incumbents from falling into an abject poverty that would discredit the whole Anglican Communion and discourage any successors, a way must be found of raising the existing minimum of £600 to the level of incomes in other comparable walks of life. No-one desires that the country clergy should live in luxury, but reasonable standards of comfort are essential if they are to do their job properly, and provide for the decent education of their children. Three possible ways of achieving this are worthy of careful study. The first is to come to some arrangement with individual parishes or groups of parishes, whereby the laity would contribute the bulk of their parson's income in exchange for a decisive voice both in his appointment and, if necessary, his dismissal. The second is to recognize frankly that the work of a country priest is only a part-time occupation, and he must expect to employ himself in secular and gainful tasks during most of the week. Finally, it would be possible, even if unpopular, to carry plurality and union to their logical conclusion in the counrtyside by forming large groupings of parishes, which would be presided over by a single rector aided by a band of assistant curates. These curates might well be celibates occupying a common clergy-house and visiting the villages on motor bicycles. Diocesan bishops are constantly appealing to their younger ordinands to postpone marriage for some years after taking orders; and since the value of the parson's wife is not as high as in the past, a celibate clergy might well be found more mobile, adaptable, and economical. Celibacy among the younger clergy is encouraged and reinforced by the growing popularity among large sections of the Anglican Communion of medieval ideals.

Inevitably in a rapidly changing world, with a bloodless social revolution at work all around her, the Church in the country is being driven either willingly or by dire necessity to build up an entirely new ecclesiastical system in the villages. Patronage, for instance, is rapidly becoming almost the sole prerogative of the Bishop-in-council. 'The position of the diocese in relation to the parochial clergy', wrote the Archdeacon of Lincoln, 'is further strengthened by the inclination of patrons to hand over their patronage to the Bishops.' But whether it is handed over or not the Bishop is nearly always consulted by private patrons, university colleges[1], or the Lord Chancellor before any appointment is made.

[1] University colleges are usually most conscientious patrons; and some of them continue to take a strongly independent line of their own.

Crown patronage of livings in any particular diocese is almost invariably placed at the disposal of its bishop, who can also prevent a nomination to any benefice for seven years, by the provisions of the *Patronage Suspension Measure*, if there are valid reasons for thinking such a step desirable, i.e. the need to link it up with others, to get rid of an over-large house, or divert some of its income into the diocesan stipends' pool.

The whole trend of modern civilization is towards centralism, bureaucracy, and the eradication of individual initiative. All three have been at work in the Church of England since the beginning of the twentieth century, and have been greatly speeded up after the second world war. They foreshadow the extinction of the traditional country parson as he has developed from the Reformation to say 1914; but they can herald the advent of another type of priest in his place; a celibate incumbent, who could administer a wide country area, work under the direct control of the Bishop, and be mobile enough to be sent where he was most needed. Above all he could be paid in accordance with either his responsibilities or his needs; and not, as at present, on the basis of a standard minimum income for each benefice, supplemented by family and car allowances. Whether such a system would appeal to the ordinary countryman is doubtful; but it should prove more efficient than the old one and certainly less financially exacting. Much, however, must necessarily depend upon the attitude of the clergy themselves. Older incumbents, who have tasted independence and appreciated the freehold, might well prefer the *ancien régime* with all its drawbacks of financial stringency. But the newly ordained men, who found it in full operation, might well feel that it represented a reasonably efficient and secure livelihood that would enhance rather than detract from their vocational powers. 'If at first sight', declared the Archdeacon of Lincoln, 'the parochial clergy appear to be losing (along with some of their grievous burdens) some of their old self-sufficiency and independence, they are gaining, through the general reinforcement of Church life in the diocese, the increasing support of the laity, and the sense of sharing in the purpose of the diocese as a whole.'

On the other hand it could be persuasively argued that individual freedom and initiative are essential if the country parson is to retain his old leadership in the village. That leadership, despite much criticism, is still self-evident and often embraces his nonconformist as well as his Anglican parishioners in all matters outside the church services. Through the parochial system, particularly perhaps in the country, national life is permeated with Christianity, and the solid work of converting the individual is carried on. Missionizing from

*The Zealous Preacher.*

outside the parish leaves little or no permanent impression upon individuals. The country parson himself is popular with and needed by his flock; largely because he lives among them as one of themselves, and they know him as a man as well as a priest. Whether the same welcome would be extended to an outsider, who enters the village merely to preach and pray and give interviews is doubtful. It is very easy for a *Times* leader-writer to state dogmatically: 'A Church living under the conditions of financial stringency which the Church of England now suffers cannot afford the luxury of confused administration. An obsession with efficiency can be fatal to freedom, but a reasonable measure of efficiency is both a condition of survival and a way of releasing energies for higher purposes.' But the human factor must also be taken into consideration. 'The level of the whole Church', wrote Canon Roger Lloyd, 'can never rise higher than the level of its parish clergy . . . it is the parish church, not the Lambeth Conference or the Church Assembly, which really makes the history of the English Church. Its rôle is decisive. The Church might possibly survive a whole generation of impossible bishops and dead cathedrals . . . it could not possibly survive a whole generation of bad vicars and lethargic parish churches. . . . The life of the parish is Church History.' It is, indeed, unlikely that the Church of the future will suffer from slack or inefficient priests; the danger lies rather in their over-zealousness. A narrow-minded rigorism in the countryside that was concerned more with liturgy, dogma, and ceremonial than with souls, might suddenly be faced by a religious revival in rural England that based itself on the Bible rather than the Prayer Book, and sought to by-pass the Establishment altogether. That would be a sorry day for the Church.

# SELECT BIBLIOGRAPHY

Addison, William, *The English Country Parson*, J. M. Dent & Sons, 1947.

Ainger, A., *Crabbe* (English Men of Letters Series), MacMillan & Co. Ltd., 1903.

Armstrong, H. B., *A Norfolk Diary*, Harrap & Co. Ltd., 1949.

Atkinson, J. C., *Forty Years in a Moorland Parish*, MacMillan & Co. Ltd., 1907.

Attwater, D., & R., *Piers Plowman*, Everyman's Library, 1957.


Babbington, Churchill, *Macaulay's Character of the Clergy*, 1849.

Baring-Gould, Sabine, *The Vicar of Morwenstow*, Methuen & Co. Ltd., 10th edn., 1933.

Bawden, E., & Carrington, N., *Life in an English Village*, Penguin Books, 1949.

Bennett, G. V., *White Kennett*, S.P.C.K., 1957.

Beresford, J., *Diary of a Country Parson*, 5 vols, Oxford University Press, 1924-1931.

Binyon, G. C., *The Christian Socialist Movement in England*, S.P.C.K., 1931.

Birchenough, C., *History of Elementary Education*, University Tutorial Press, 1938.

Bradley, A. G., *Exmoor Memories*, Methuen & Co. Ltd., 1926.
　　　　　　　　*Our Centenarian Grandfather*, Bale Brothers Ltd., 1924.

Brookes, F. W., 'The Social Position of the Parson in the Sixteenth Century', *Journal of the British Archaeological Association*, Third Series, Vol. X, 1945-1947.

Brown, C. K. F., *A History of the English Clergy 1800-1900*, Faith Press Ltd., 1938

Brown, C. K. F., *The Church's Part in Education*, S.P.C.K., 1942.

Brown, J. R., *Number One, Millbank*, S.P.C.K., 1944.

Burgess, H. J., *Enterprise in Education*, S.P.C.K., 1957.

Byles, C. E., *The Life and Letters of R. S. Hawker*, Lane, 1905.


Carpenter, E. F., *The Protestant Bishop*, Longmans, Green & Co. Ltd., 1956.

Carpenter, S. C., *Church and People*, S.P.C.K., 1933.

*Chaucer's Canterbury Tales for the Modern Reader*, Everyman's Library, 1930.

Christmas, F. E., *The Parson in English Literature*, Hodder & Stoughton Ltd., 1950.

Clive, M., *Caroline Clive*, Bodley Head Ltd., 1949.

Cobbett, William, *Legacy to Parsons*, 1869.

Collins, J. Churton, *An English Garner: Critical Essays and Literary Fragments*, 1903.

Combe, W., *Tours of Dr Syntax*, 1812.

Coombs, H., and Bax, A. N., *Journal of a Somerset Rector*, John Murray Ltd., 1930.

Coulton, G. G., *Life in the Middle Ages*, Vols I & II, Cambridge University Press, 1928.
                    *The Medieval Village*, Cambridge University Press, 1925.
                    *Medieval Panorama*, Cambridge University Press, 1938.

Cowper, William, *Poetical Works*, 1851.

Cragg, G. R., *Puritanism in the Period of the Great Persecution*, Cambridge University Press, 1957.

Cragg, W. A., *Tales of a Lincolnshire Antiquary*, W. Morton & Sons 1949.

Cropper, Margaret, *Flame Touches Flame*, Longmans, Green & Co. Ltd., 1951.

Cutts, E. L., *Parish Priests and Their People in the Middle Ages In England*, 1898.


Daubeney, A. G., *Reminiscences of a Country Parson*, The Griffen Press, 1950.

Davies, E. W. L., *Memoir of Revd John Russell*, 1883.

Ditchfield, P. H., *Old-Time Parson*, Methuen & Co. Ltd., 1908.

Driver, Cecil, *Tory Radical*, Oxford University Press, 1947.


Ellman, E. B., *Recollections of a Sussex Parson*, Combridges, 1912.


Fisher, J. F., *The Harlow Deanery*, Benham & Co. Ltd., 1922.

Forbes, G. M., *George Herbert's Country Parson*, Faith Press, 1949.

Forrest, A. J., *Village Cricket*, Robert Hale Ltd., 1957.


Garbett, C., *The Church and State in England*, Hodder & Stoughton Ltd., 1950.

Goddard, F., *Reminiscences of a Wiltshire Vicar*, printed but unpublished, 1887.

Hart, A. Tindal, *The Country Clergy in Elizabethan and Stuart Times*, Phoenix House Ltd., 1958.
    *The Eighteenth Century Country Parson*, Wilding & Sons Ltd., 1955.
    *Life and Times of John Sharp, Archibshop of York*, S.P.C.K., 1949.
    *William Lloyd*, S.P.C.K., 1952.
Hart, A. Tindal, and Carpenter, E. F., *The Nineteenth Century Country Parson*, Wilding & Son Ltd., 1954.
Hill, Christopher, *Economic Problems of the Church*, Oxford University Press, 1956.
Hilton, R. H., and Fagan, H., *The English Rising of 1381*, Lawrence & Wishart, 1950.
Hole, S. R., *Memoirs of Dean Hole*,1893.
    *More Memoirs of Dean Hole*, 1894.
Hopkinson, A. W., *Pastor's Progress*, Michael Joseph Ltd., 1942.
Hoskins, W. G., 'The Leicestershire Country Parson in the Sixteenth Century', *Leicestershire Archaeological Society*, Vol. XXI, 1940.

Jarvis, Kathleen, *The Impressions of a Parson's Wife*, Mowbray & Co. Ltd., 1951.
Jones, M. G., *The Charity School Movement*, Cambridge University Press, 1937.

Ketton-Cremer, R. W., *Country Neighbourhood*, Faber & Faber Ltd., 1951.

Law, William, *A Serious Call to a Devout and Holy Life*, S.P.C.K. edn. 1905.
Leach, A. F., *The Schools of Medieval England*, Methuen & Co. Ltd., 1915.
Linnell, C. D., (ed.) *The Diary of Benjamin Rogers*, Bedford Historical Record Society, 1949.
Lloyd, Roger, *The Church of England in the Twentieth Century*, 2 vols, Longmans, Green & Co. Ltd., 1946.

Marson, Charles, *Village Silhouettes*, Society of SS. Peter and Paul, edn. 1930.
Martin, E. W., *The Secret People*, Phoenix House Ltd., 1954.
Matthews, A. G., *Walker Revised*, Oxford University Press, 1948.
Mayfield, Guy, *The Church of England: its Members and its Business*, Oxford University Press, 1958.
Meadows, D., *Elizabethan Quintet*, 1956.

Moorman, J. R. H., *A History of the Church in England*, A. & C.
        Black Ltd., 1953.
        *Church Life in England in the Thirteenth
        Century*, Cambridge University Press, 1945.

Noel, Conrad, *An Autobiography*, ed. Sydney Dark, J. M. Dent &
Sons Ltd., 1945.

Ollard, S. L., and Walker, P. C., *Archbishop Herring's Visitation
Returns*, 5 vols, Yorkshire Archaeological Society, 1928.
Owst, G. R., *Preaching in Medieval England*, Cambridge Univer-
        sity Press, 1926.
        *Literature and Pulpit in Medieval England*, Cam-
        bridge University Press, 1933.

Pearson, Hesketh, *The Smith of Smiths*, Hamish Hamilton Ltd.,
1934.
Pickard-Cambridge, A. W., *Memorial of the Revd Octavius Pickard-
Cambridge*, privately printed, 1918.
Plomer, William, *Diary of the Revd Francis Kilvert*, 3 vols, Jonathan
Cape Ltd., 1938-1940.
Ponsonby, Arthur, *English Diaries*, Methuen & Co. Ltd., 1923.
                *More English Diaries*, Methuen & Co. Ltd.,
                1927.
Powys, A. R., *The English Parish Church*, Longmans, U.S.A., 1930.
Purcell, W. E., *Onward Christian Soldier*, Longmans, Green & Co.
Ltd., 1957.
Purvis, J. S., *Tudor Parish Documents*, Cambridge University Press
1948.

Reckitt, M. B., *Maurice to Temple*, Faber & Faber Ltd., 1947.
Royds, T. F., *Haughton Rectory*, Wilding & Son Ltd., 1953.

Skrine, J. H. *Pastor Ovium*, Longmans, Green & Co. Ltd., 1909.
Smyth, Charles, *Church and Parish*, S.P.C.K., 1955.
Stokes, F. G., *Bletcheley Diary of the Revd William Cole*, Constable
& Co. Ltd., 1931.

Tawney, R. H., *Religion and the Rise of Capitalism*, John Murray,
1927.
Thompson, A. Hamilton, *Visitations in the Diocese of Lincoln
1517-1531*, Lincoln Record Society, 1940.
Thompson, Flora, *Lark Rise to Candleford:* a trilogy, Oxford
University Press, 1945.
Thompson, H. P., *Thomas Bray*, S.P.C.K., 1954.

Venn, J. A., *The Foundations of Agricultural Economics*, Cambridge University Press, 1933.

Wagner, D. O., *The Church of England and Social Reform since 1854*, Columbia University Press, 1930.

Wake, Joan, *A Northamptonshire Rector*, Archer & Goodman, 1943.

Wakefield, G. S., *Puritan Devotion*, Epworth Press, 1957.

Warner, James, Lee, *Parochialia* (unpublished).

Watt, M. H., *The History of the Parson's Wife*, Faber & Faber Ltd., 1943.

West, F. H., *Rude Forefathers*, Bannisdale Press, 1949.
         *Sparrows of the Spirit*, privately printed for the Nottinghamshire Historic Churches Funds, 1957.

Wingfield-Stratford, E., *This Was a Man*, Robert Hale Ltd., 1949.

# INDEX

Headbourne Worthy, Hants., 73
Helmingham, Suffolk, 44
Hemmingstone, Suffolk, 44
Henchman, Humphrey, Bishop, 81
Henley-on-Thames, Oxon., 129
Henry VIII, 67, 113
Henslow, John Stevens, 38, 49, 60, 74, 146
Herbert, George, 17, 30, 31, 33, 44, 73, 76, 108, 132, 133, 145
Herne, Kent, 95
Herrick, Robert, 76, 133
Herring, Archbishop, 46
Hessle, Yorks., 88
Heyford, Northants., 73
High Wych, Herts., 96, 139, 142
Hildyard, James, 77
Hilmarton, Wilts., 142
Hitcham, Suffolk, 38, 49, 60, 74, 146
Holdich, John, 82
Holmes, Joseph, 141
Hooker, Richard, 37, 73, 131
Hopkinson, A. W., 66
Horsted Keynes, Sussex, 80
Huddersfield, Yorks., 35
Hudson, Michael, 89
Hull, Yorks., 88
Hullavington, Wilts., 78
Hungarton, Leics., 132
Hursley, Hants., 73
Hutcheson, Mrs, 32

Ilkley, Yorks., 86
Ingoldsby, Lincs., 77
Ingoldsby, Thomas, 76
Ipswich, Suffolk, 74
Isle of Man, 83

Jackson, Bishop, 138
James I, 67
James II, 68
Johnson, Frank, 139
Johnson, Samuel, 74
Jones, Richard, 88

Jones, Septimus, 98
Jones, Thomas, 89, 137
Jones, William, 82, 92, 119, 138
Josselin, Ralph, 80, 118, 135

Kaye, Bishop, 138
Keble, John, 66, 73
Ken, Thomas, 39
Kenneth, Bishop, 89
Kennett, White, 37, 44, 73, 83
Kett, Robert, 67
Kettlewell, Yorks., 86
Ketsby, Lincs., 154
Kidderminster, Worcs., 80, 81
Kilvert, Francis, 76, 79, 98
King, Edward, 103
King's Cliffe, Northants., 32, 54, 143
King's Somborne, Hants., 50
King's Sutton, Northants., 132
Kingsley, Charles, 38, 47, 58, 64, 65, 66, 73, 76, 92, 97
Kingston-on-Thames, Surrey, 129
Kinwarton, Worcs., 33, 50, 60, 91, 96, 145
Kirby Underdale, Yorks., 73
Kirkheaton, Yorks., 86
Kirton, Notts., 42
Kirton-in-Lindsay, Lincs., 77
Knowstone, Devon, 93, 104
Knyghtley, Matthew, 130, 131, 132

Lang, Cosmo, Archbishop, 95
Langar, Notts., 79, 89, 104
Langland, William, 14, 16, 37, 41, 72, 92, 105, 111, 112
Latton, Essex, 95
Laud, William, 28, 106, 113, 115
Lavington, Suffolk, 33
Law, William, 30, 32, 33
Laxton, Northants., 103
Layng, William, 53
Leadenham, Lincs., 101, 133
Leasingham, Lincs., 77
Leband, Robert, 79
Leigh, Hon. J. W., 69
Leintwardine, Herefordshire, 61

Penrose, Thomas, 79
Penrose, Mary, 79
Perkins, William, 34
Perry, G. G., 77
Peterborough, Northants., 137
Pett, Thomas, 100
Phillpotts, Henry, 93, 94
Philpot, Benjamin, 83, 84, 95, 109
Pickard, Thomas, 87
Pickard-Cambridge, Octavius, 76
Pickford, Francis, 110
Pilgrimage of Grace, 67
Poor Law Amendment Act 1834, 59, 63
Portsmouth, Hants., 91
Powell, George, 36
Preist, Thomas, 86, 97
Prestwick, Lancs., 134

Queen Anne, 18, 124
Queen Anne's Bounty, 111, 119, 120, 123, 124, 139

Rackham, Horace, 96, 142
Radwinter, Essex, 81, 106, 129
Raikes, Robert, 47
Ramsey, James, 62, 63
Rapsley, Lincs., 154
Ravens, Jeremiah, 103
Redbourn, Herts., 94
Redman, Bishop, 45, 109
Revesby, Lincs., 77
Richard II, 40
Rippingale, Lincs., 133, 154
Ritson, C., 49
Rogers, Benjamin, 82, 108, 109
Rolleston, Notts., 79
Rotherfield, Sussex, 97
Routh, Roger, 132
Russell, Jack, 94
Russell, Lord John, 48, 59
Rustat, William, 130

Sacheverell, Dr, 68
St Alban's, Herts., 57
St Augustine, 84
St Clair, Patrick, 82

Sale, T. W., 77
Salisbury, Wilts., 48, 62, 73
Salmonby, Lincs., 154
Sampson, William, 79, 97
Saperton, Lincs., 154
Sawbridgeworth, Herts., 139, 141
Schrivelsby, Lincs., 77
Selborne, Hants., 74
Seymour, Richard, 33, 37, 50, 60, 87, 91, 96, 98, 145
Shaftesbury, Lord, 62
Sheldon, Gilbert, Archbishop, 117
Sheldon, Warws., 45
Ship Money, 117
Shipmeadow, Suffolk, 150
Shottesbrooke, Berks., 37, 44, 83
Simon, Peter, 62
Skinner, John, 78, 82
Skipton, Yorks., 86
Slater, William, 106
Smarden, Kent, 87, 88
Smith, Sydney, 58, 59, 93, 96, 104, 109, 110, 139, 140, 141
Snargate, Kent, 76
Somerby, Leics., 92, 106
Somerby, Lincs., 154
Somersby, Lincs., 79, 154
Spalding, Lincs., 77
S.P.C.K., 45, 47
Springfield, Essex, 83
Stamford, Lincs., 87
Stanhope, Henry, 103
Star Chamber, 106
Steele, Richard, 18
Sterne, Laurence, 76, 146
Steventon, Hants., 79
Stock, Thomas, 47
Stockton, Warws., 38, 65, 91
Stokes, Edward, 94
Stoneleigh, Warws., 69
Stratford, John, 105
Stratford St Andrew, Suffolk, 102
Sudbury, Archbishop, 56, 57
Sustead, Norfolk, 82, 102
Sutton, F. H., 77

Sutton-on-the-Forest, Yorks., 146

Swinstead, Lincs., 141

Swymbridge, Devon, 94

Sylvester, Edward, 147

Takeley, Essex, 49, 96, 142, 146

Tarrant Gunville, Dorset, 50, 61, 97

Taunton, Somerset, 109, 139

Taylor, Jeremy, 31, 32, 33

Teasdale, Thomas, 78

Teddington, Middlesex, 74

Temple, Frederick, 94

Ten Hours Bill, 63

Tenison, Thomas, 45

Tennyson, Lord, 79

Terrott, C. P., 77

Terry, John, 87, 88

Teston, Kent, 62

Tetford, Lincs., 154

Thaxted, Essex, 66

Theodore, Archbishop, 13

Thorpe, Yorks., 136

Thorpe-on-the-Hill, Lincs., 130

Tildersley, Tristram, 90

Tithe Acts, 123

Tithe Commutation Act, 122

Tithe Redemption Act, 20, 124

Tockenham, Wilts., 53

Tolpuddle Martyrs, 63

Towersey, Bucks., 88

Townsend, T. J. M., 77

Trentislow, Devon, 147

Tressilian, Justice, 57

Trollope, Bishop, 77

Truro, Cornwall, 35

Trustees for Maintenance, 114, 118

Tuckwell, F. W., 38, 58, 65, 66, 91

Tufnell, E. W., 146

Tyler, Wat., 56

Uffington, Lincs., 89

Underwood, William, 86

Uppingham, Rutland, 31

Upton-near-Southwell, Notts., 134

Upton-upon-Seven, Worcs., 101

Venn, Henry, 35

Wade, Arthur, 63

Wade, John, 81, 82

Waddington, Lincs., 77

Wake, William, 119

Walpole, Horace, 82

Walker, Samuel, 35

Walkeringham, Notts., 49

Waller, William, 89

Walter, John, 59

Waltham Cross, Essex, 73

Walton, Isaac, 30

Warehorne, Kent, 76

Warkworth, Northants., 73

Warmington, Northants., 128, 140

Warner, James Lee, 50, 61, 79, 97

Warrington, Lancs., 64

Wartling, Sussex, 48

Warwick, 63

Waterloo, Battle of, 18, 79, 89

Watson, Joshua, 47

Wattkinson, Robert, 109

Wellingborough, Northants., 141

Wesley, John, 33, 62, 87

Wesley, Samuel, 73, 83, 138

Wesley, Susannah, 73, 144

West Dean, Sussex, 128

Weston Longueville, Norfolk, 80

Whatley, Somerset, 17, 33

White, George, 87, 89

White, Gilbert, 74, 75

Whitkirk, Yorks., 86

White Roothing, Essex, 76, 110

Wilberforce, William, 62, 63

William III, 83, 133

Williams, Roland, 48

Winchester, Hants., 28, 40, 73

Winchfield, Hants., 66

Windermere, Westmorland, 37